The
ENTREPRENEURIAL
CULTURE

23 Ways To Engage and Empower Your People

The ENTREPRENEURIAL CULTURE

23 Ways To Engage and Empower Your People

Michael Houlihan & Bonnie Harvey

Authors of the *New York Times* Bestseller *The Barefoot Spirit*

Founders of Barefoot, America's #1 Wine Brand

The content of this book has been prepared for informational purposes only. Although anyone may find the ideas, concepts, practices, suggestions, recommendations, disciplines, and understandings presented in this book to be useful, the contents of this book are provided with the understanding that neither the author nor the publisher is engaged in providing any specific business advice to the reader. Nor is anything in this book intended to be a strategy or recommendation for any specific kind of business problem or business opportunity. Each person and business has unique needs, qualities, resources, abilities, and other attributes and this book cannot take these individual differences into account. Each person and business should engage a qualified professional to address his, her, or its unique situation.

"THE ENTREPRENEURIAL CULTURE: 23 Ways to Engage and Empower Your People"

Published by Footnotes Press, LLC

Cover design by Brad Metzgar *(metzgardesign.com)* based on original cover design for *The Barefoot Spirit* by Brand Navigation *(brandnavigation.com)* inspired by original cover concept by Thomas Anderson *(209designshop.com)*
Cover illustration by Jef Gunion *(guniondesign.com)*
Author photographs and back cover photograph by Robert Pierce *(rpstudios.com)*

978-0-9907937-0-0 paperback
978-0-9907937-1-7 ePUB

Printed in the United States of America

10 9 8 7 6 5 4 3 2 1

Complimentary
Business Resources

The free companion items to this book, including video demonstrations, webinars, lesson guides, printable versions of handouts, and updates are available at:

TheBarefootSpirit.com/Culture

Please access these additional resources, as they are available for a limited time.

Book an entrepreneurial culture keynote, workshop, or corporate training session today at TheBarefootSpirit.com/BookUs.

For Michael's mentor, Keith Murdoch, former city manager of Anaheim, California, and former president of the League of California Cities

Keith hired Michael as an intern right out of college and later made him an assistant. Keith gave Michael extensive responsibility and guidance, and first introduced him to the importance and power of entrepreneurial cultures. Keith ran his municipal corporation with an exciting entrepreneurial culture that engaged his people and empowered them to do great things. Under Keith and his team, Anaheim became a model for the rest of the country. The city created its own municipal water and power companies, servicing other cities in Orange County. It attracted Disneyland, built the Anaheim Stadium, created a unique lease-back arrangement to finance the Anaheim Convention Center, and annexed and developed the Santa Ana Canyon, doubling the size of the city—all of which was conceptualized and executed by Keith's own people, whom he constantly encouraged, acknowledged, and publicly appreciated. Michael is honored to have had the opportunity to work with Keith.

Contents

	Foreword	xi
	Acknowledgments	xix
	Introduction	xxi
Chapter One	Teach employees to think like owners by scaling down to two divisions	1
Chapter Two	Hire for hustle	5
Chapter Three	Don't skimp on training	9
Chapter Four	Use performance-based compensation, and share the wealth	13
Chapter Five	Get out of your employees' way	17
Chapter Six	Delegate effectively	21
Chapter Seven	Let information flow freely	25
Chapter Eight	Don't wait for perfectly sunny conditions to allow employees to take the initiative on a project	33
Chapter Nine	Ask a lot of questions	35

Chapter Ten	Never waste a perfectly good mistake	39
Chapter Eleven	The ball is always in your court	43
Chapter Twelve	Make sure you're solving the right problems	49
Chapter Thirteen	Learn to extrapolate	55
Chapter Fourteen	Know the difference between customer service and complaint resolution	59
Chapter Fifteen	There's no substitute for face-to-face relationships	63
Chapter Sixteen	Make organization a priority	67
Chapter Seventeen	Get serious about time management	73
Chapter Eighteen	Always over-deliver	79
Chapter Nineteen	Always ask yourself, "How would I like it?"	83
Chapter Twenty	The customer buys *you* more than your product	89
Chapter Twenty-One	Don't take "no" for an answer	93
Chapter Twenty-Two	Say "thank you" to everyone— especially to your employees	97
Chapter Twenty-Three	Make it fun to work for you	101
	Resources	106
	About the Authors	120

Foreword

By Jeffrey Hayzlett

Companies that do great things get great results, and companies that don't do great things don't get great results. It's just the way of the business world. Companies destined to survive long-term are able to read the nuances of the industry and respond to change with quick, confident (and smart) decisions. They take risks when growth opportunities arise. They are perpetually restless, ever watchful, always thinking a step or two ahead.

The "whys" are pretty self-evident: the complexities of globalization, the frenetic pace of technology, the quicksand whims of the marketplace, the endless army of competitors vying for position. Money is a factor, too. It helps, but I have seen some well-heeled, deep-pocketed companies fail. We have all seen it: Oceans of capital (or at least credit) covered a multitude of sins, but these forgiving waters have long since receded.

All of this is highly problematic for most big corporations. The management structure and the policies that have kept them stable and thriving for decades have now become liabilities. They get "corporate." You know, they move at the speed of a slug, and that's just not fast enough. They get bogged down in endless paperwork and seem to think the act of having a meeting is more important than the purpose of the meeting.

We are in a new age. The upshot is that corporations forged to meet the "command and control" needs of the Industrial Age must now create cultures in which employees don't act like employees at all, but like entrepreneurs. Everyone must be engaged (tuned in enough to see problems and motivated enough to solve them) and empowered (so they *can* solve them). See it? Fix it, now.

Michael Houlihan and Bonnie Harvey, authors of this book and founders of the bestselling Barefoot Wine brand, say that all road-blocks to employee engagement and empowerment originate in the three "sacred cows" of corporate culture:

- Corporate structure: Rigid divisions of labor can create turf battles and stifle communication and innovation.

- Compliance: Lawyers tend to want *everything* to run through compliance. Sometimes the wait for legal approval on a new initiative is so long that people just run out of steam.

- Compensation: Paying for attendance rather than production leads to mediocrity. High producers are likely to leave when they realize they're being paid the same as the clock watchers and net surfers who contribute the bare minimum.

I agree. To these new enemies, I toast them and quote Shake-speare, "Cry 'havoc!' and let slip the dogs of war." Companies *do* need to take a close look at all three areas and ask themselves the hard questions. Only then will they be able to begin to transform their cultures over time.

And yes, culture change *does* take time. Lots of it. That's why it's called culture. Want to impact organizations, fast? Focus on "mood." A company's mood can actually change pretty quickly, and I've found changing it is the first step toward changing culture.

While a bit oversimplified, a "bad mood" reflects the attitude that your company's best days are in the past. You don't want your employees believing that! You want them to believe that your best days lie ahead—and that they have a strong personal stake in helping reach those days. Where these conditions are met you find a "good mood." Sometimes it's so good you can feel an underlying hum of energy when you look around at everyone.

You might call that good mood the entrepreneurial spirit. Bonnie and Michael call it "the Barefoot Spirit" (which, incidentally, is also the title of their excellent first book).

I have bought and sold over 250 companies and worked with many others in a variety of ways during my career. Through it all I've seen more than my share of "bad moods" up close and personal. Here are just a few of the big mistakes I've seen companies make:

They force people to follow rigid rules that don't make any sense. While I was at one company we needed 12 new chairs for the conference room. Unfortunately, there was a rule that we couldn't order 12 chairs at a time. However, we could order six chairs—so to get around it we had to place two orders of six.

Okay, yes: By itself this was not insurmountable. It wasn't *that* hard to solve the chair-ordering dilemma. Yet when you have big lists of things employees can't do you force them to burn up their innovative thinking on workarounds and trivial problems. Plus, it's incredibly frustrating. Good people don't want to work in this kind of environment.

They set up obstacles to employee effectiveness. When I worked in big corporations they sometimes had rules that prevented employees from using, say, iPods or iPhones at work. It was typically a security issue. Yet some people found they could be more effective and efficient using these prohibited tools, and so they started working from two devices: one for the workplace and one for home.

I'm not trying to address the question of whether people can be more efficient working at home. Sometimes they can. What I *am* saying is that it makes no sense to create a work environment where people can't do their best work. It just isn't smart. And it certainly doesn't lend itself to entrepreneurialism.

They build policies around a lack of trust. Now I'm going to tell you a story about Kodak, where I served as Chief Marketing Officer from 2009 to 2010. (I have a lot of respect for Kodak so I am not slamming it or trying to single it out. This anecdote just happens to be a good illustration of what I'm trying to say here.)

Anyway, I wanted to change the business cards. The cards had people's photos on them, which I loved, but the photos had not been updated in years. They were taken when people first joined the company, and since the average length of employment was 27 years, it was time to re-do them. So I wanted to let everyone put any photo they wanted on the back of the card, along with a personalized branding statement.

The point is that they wouldn't let me do it. Legal basically said, "Jeff, we can't let you do this because what if someone puts something inappropriate on their card?" My response was, "First of all, I'd hope no one would ever think to do that. Second, if they did, it would just help us find out exactly where the stupid people are."

This policy was set up to control the possible handful of people who can't be trusted at the expense of the people who can. When you consider the level of trust that an entrepreneurial culture requires, you can see the problem. If you can't trust someone not to put "I'm a non-stop sex machine" on the back of their business card, how can you ever trust them to make decisions that affect the future of your company?

They shut down disagreement. In an entrepreneurial culture you don't just allow disagreement, you invite it. You're looking for autonomy and creative thinking, and of course that can't happen in an environment where the boss's word always prevails. Yet so many times I've seen employees share ideas that are ignored or even aggressively shot down because the boss disagrees. Leaders should encourage tension as they drive change and let employees shine when they rise to the challenge.

Let people experience that a few times and they get the message pretty quickly: Toe the party line. And—of course—they do. Smart people don't keep fighting a losing battle.

The real problem, of course, is that no one has all the answers. Good leaders know this. And it's not a reluctant knowledge. They like not having all the answers because they get to learn something new. And that's exciting.

They discourage risk taking. I like to talk about the three seconds of fear that stand between not doing something and doing it. We all feel fear, and that's good. Tension is good for us. It stretches us. Fear, for the most part, means something exciting is in the works. But when those three seconds always end with us pulling back, cowering down, turning tail—whatever cliché you want—the exciting thing never happens. That's when a company stagnates. Embrace the change!

Entrepreneurs are inherent risk takers. If they let the fear win every time they wouldn't be entrepreneurs. There are times, of course, when the decision is no—when it *should* be no. But when leaders *never* take risks, and when they *never* let employees take risks, their culture is the opposite of entrepreneurial. Apathy sets in. People don't try anything new and so they don't fail—until, of course, one day the whole enterprise fails spectacularly.

Despite years of lip service to the contrary, they still embrace silo thinking. Have you noticed some companies are now putting in offices of innovation? What the hell is that? We've heard *ad nauseam* about the evils of the silo mentality where different parts of the company never communicate with each other, but the notion that innovation is an "office" takes silo-ing to a whole new level.

The spirit of innovation must flow freely throughout an organization, finding its way like an underground stream. Trying to compartmentalize it shows that too many leaders don't get how culture works. The ability and willingness to innovate—like self-motivation, flexibility, great communication skills, and other aspects of the entrepreneurial mindset—has to be organic. It can never be assigned or imposed but must arise, naturally, as a result of policies and practices that invite it.

The great news is that you *can* change the mood of your company. But the turnaround really does need to happen from the ground up. And you can't snap your fingers and say, "Okay, let's all become entrepreneurial now!" (If only it were so easy!) However, there *are* certain concrete things you can do to encourage that spirit to flourish.

The Entrepreneurial Culture covers many such tactics. I believe they can help you transform your company. Not only is this book a product of the brilliant minds that created a bestselling wine brand despite having no money and no industry experience, it's written for maximum impact.

What you'll love about this book:

- It's very specific and tactical. It tells you exactly what to do to start transforming your culture right now. Rather than bogging you down with a lot of theory, the authors get to the point with tactics you can put in place right away.

- It's filled with great anecdotes that bring the material to life and help you visualize success in your own endeavor.

- The chapters are short and digestible. The book is a quick and easy read for a company's entire leadership team.

Bottom line: This is a book that will really get read. What's more, the ideas are doable. When something feels doable you're more likely to do it. And when you do it—well, I'm hardly the first person to point out that life rewards action. Yet I'm going to add my voice to the chorus: It does.

Lastly, I'd like to address a final fear that might be nagging at you. You may be wondering if, despite all the changes you might put in place, your employees really have what it takes to become entrepreneurial thinkers and doers. Let me assure you: They *do*.

Lately I've heard a lot of talk about generational differences in regard to work ethic (specifically, a lack of it), the need for a lot of hand-holding, a distressing sense of entitlement, and so on. I don't believe it and I hope you don't either.

From everything I have observed, nothing has changed about human nature. And the basics of good business are still the basics. With the proper motivation and the right systems and processes, we can all bring out the best in our people. We can turn average employees into good ones, and good employees into great ones.

Great employees still want to do great work. Our job as leaders is to get out of their way and let them do it.

Acknowledgments

We give our heartfelt thanks to these people for their help and support:

Jeff Hayzlett, who inspired us to share what we know about the immense power of entrepreneurial cultures with C-Suite leaders.

Dottie DeHart, who encouraged us and helped us see how valuable our lessons on entrepreneurship could be for today's corporations.

The DeHart & Company writing team—Anna Campbell, Lindsay Miller, and Meghan Waters—who helped with structuring, copywriting, and proofreading.

The Barefoot Spirit team, who squeezed considerable extra work into their already busy schedules to make this book possible.

Introduction

Companies search high and low for the competitive advantage that will give them a leg up in today's chaotic and uncertain business world. But many never find it. Why? Because they're looking in the wrong place. If you want a company that can withstand the dips and slips of today's market, you have to look within...at your employees.

Take a close look. Who exactly is darkening your company's doors every day? Are they enthusiasm fakers, paycheck collectors, and clock watchers? Or are they people who truly feel like they have a stake in your company's success? It's really up to you.

Despite the chaos and uncertainty, this is a time of extreme opportunity for companies that recognize the value of entrepreneurial thinking. It is by far one of the greatest competitive advantages for companies today, and not just at the top of organizations, but at every level, from the bottom up. When you get your employees to think like owners, it will solve the biggest problem in business right now—lack of engagement. Once they see the difference they can make, everything will change. They'll be excited to be part of the process.

Employees who think like "owners" and who are truly engaged are *more productive, more creative, more loyal, and have a proven positive impact on the bottom line*. Keep in mind, too, that the people closest to the problems in organizations are often the best ones to solve them. When employees think like owners, you can tackle obstacles before they become costly and cumbersome.

The trouble is that many companies try to infuse entrepreneurial thinking into a culture that's fundamentally flawed. It won't work. Getting employees to think and act like entrepreneurs is a natural, organic extension of a company's culture, and people can't be cajoled, tricked, or bribed into doing it. There just aren't any shortcuts.

When we started Barefoot Cellars, we learned early on that our growth and success depended on our employees: how hard they worked, the ideas they had, how committed they were when times got tough, the types of relationships they formed with customers, and so much more. Keeping our employees inspired and happy, and honestly acknowledging how much we appreciated their loyalty and efforts, were some of our top priorities as business owners.

And they should be every C-Suiter's top priorities. For us, entrepreneurial thinking is no longer just a "nice thing to have" for organizations; we think the survival of today's organizations depends on it. That's why we've created *The Entrepreneurial Culture*.

We like to think of Barefoot as a modern entrepreneurial success story, and with this book, we're sharing how we kept the spirit of entrepreneurship alive in our company. It wonderfully complements the lessons from our *New York Times* Bestseller *The Barefoot Spirit: How Hardship, Hustle, and Heart Built America's #1 Wine Brand* and is every 21st Century leader's guide to infusing their company culture with entrepreneurial thinking.

Throughout *The Entrepreneurial Culture*, you'll find advice on how to grow and nurture entrepreneurial thinking in your employees. In chapters on hiring, embracing mistakes, fostering innovation, and much, much more, you'll learn how to turn a company of clock watchers into a company of doers who feel empowered, appreciated, and free to innovate—all while the employees and the organization reap the immense benefits that come with it.

We kept it short and sweet on purpose. We took the best ideas and distilled them down to a quick, easy-to-read primer. It's the perfect size for you and your employees—whether they're in the C-Suite, frontline managers, or new hires—to read without being overwhelmed so they'll be ready to be active participants in bringing an entrepreneurial culture to life at your organization.

Let's get started.

Chapter One

Teach employees to think like owners by scaling down to two divisions

As a C-Suite leader, you're hyper-focused on your company's productivity, profits, and growth. Wouldn't it be nice if your employees were as focused on those factors as you and the company's other executives? Sure, they do what you tell them. They come in every day and perform every task within their job descriptions. But often that's where the buck stops. If a problem lands in their laps that isn't what they consider to be "their responsibility," they pass it on to the next guy or they bring it to you expecting a solution.

But it doesn't have to be that way. You can teach your employees to think and act outside of their job descriptions—to think, in point of fact, like owners! At Barefoot Cellars, we found that the key to turning worker bees into solutions-oriented entrepreneurs was simplifying our structure into just two divisions: sales and sales support.

The reasoning behind this decision is simple: Everyone in your company gets paid from sales. Without sales, there is simply no money to pay salaries, bonuses, or benefits. Ergo, sales are the target every employee should be aiming for, and the goal everyone should be supporting. So even though they each have important, specific functions to perform, your employees in production, accounting, marketing, legal, and so on are ultimately sales support.

If you don't make a few more changes in how your company operates, though, splitting your company into these two divisions will be worthless.

First, make sure every single person in sales support knows how his or her job affects sales. When non-sales employees are too isolated and don't have a big-picture view of how your company operates, even their well-meaning suggestions and efforts are likely to be unhelpful. For instance, a suggestion to decrease production time might ultimately affect the quality of your product. Or a promising computer projection might not accurately reflect conditions in the field. Or even a new piece of marketing material (that everyone in marketing loves!) may not be practical at the retail level.

Specifically, watch out for these five phrases, which often preface well-meant but unhelpful suggestions from sales support people:

- *"Why don't we just…?"* This is how suggestions to cut costs usually start. The suggestion itself indicates that the speaker doesn't know why we "don't just." A thoughtful discussion will usually result in many answers to this ageless question.

- *"Why do we have to…?"* This is usually followed by a suggestion to make the speaker's job easier, thus reducing labor costs. This question may indicate that the employee doesn't really know or understand why they must do this or that. There are many subtle quality indicators and nuances in your product or package that they may not realize exist, but that give your product the edge in the market.

- *"If we just cut this out, we could save…"* and then, they do the math. This is usually a simple multiple of a small savings times the number of units sold. Beware! This line of thinking assumes that sales will at least stay the same, or even increase. (And you know what they say about assuming.) The truth is, isolated money-saving ideas may hurt sales in ways that the employee knows nothing about. Keep in mind that savings are rarely as simple as a mathematical formula. By discussing the need for what your employee suggests cutting, you will both come to a better understanding of what is necessary to make sales happen.

- *"I just came up with this great idea!"* Some suggestions stem from your people's desire to make their mark on your product or package. Sometimes their motive is career, sometimes it's based on a desire to be more like your competition, or they may think, "It's time for a change." Whatever the case may be, though, remember that your product's uniqueness may be the very advantage that distinguishes it in the marketplace. Consistent packaging and logo designs are critical to your product's image of dependability. When it comes to effective change, the watchword is evolution, not revolution.

- *"This will increase sales."* What your marketing people design on their computer screens may look fine to them, but until it has it been field-tested, whether or not it will "work" is an unknown. Marketing is expensive, so think carefully before funds are spent on a new idea.

Secondly, find a way to link pay for sales support to the performance of sales. When we began giving our sales support people bonuses based on quarterly sales amounts, the entire office began actively rooting for the salespeople who were roaming the country, because their paychecks depended on their colleagues' success! In short order, Barefoot became more efficient, more responsive, and even closer-knit. Instead of moving forward in separate boats, our employees were now on the same ship. They knew that they all needed to row together—and they did!

For instance, if a salesperson in Michigan needed statistics to convince a store owner to place an order, the office staff hustled out a report. If our crew needed signs and posters for an event in Seattle, the marketing folks jumped right on it. If Barefoot won a gold medal in Orange County, staffers made sure shelf signs were printed and in the hands of Southern California Barefooters the next day. Income was at stake for everyone.

Owner-like thinking happened on a smaller scale, too. Our people began to look for everyday ways to save time and money, like holding off using the color copier if they didn't really need it.

We think you'll see similar results if you commit to a two-division model, and ensure that each employee's salary is directly affected by the success of sales. One last piece of advice: Be sure to support owner-like thinking in your company by creating a culture of permission, in which your employees feel free to experiment, take chances, and even make legitimate mistakes as they seek to come up with out-of-the-box solutions and innovative improvements.

Chapter Two

Hire for hustle

How can you make sure you're hiring people who will help your company grow and thrive? Here's our advice: Hire people you like who have foundational qualities you can build on, such as integrity, enthusiasm, a willingness to learn, initiative, a sense of humor, and a sincere interest in your company, to name a few.

And keep in mind that you absolutely can tell from the hiring process whether someone is an entrepreneurial thinker who will add to the culture you're building. A great way to separate the entrepreneurial thinkers from those who aren't is to place a special emphasis on hiring people with a sense of urgency; people who can and will move quickly; people who don't always have to be told what their next step should be.

In other words, don't hire solely based on someone's technical skill set. You can always teach that. You can't teach the other stuff—and that other stuff is what will make the difference between an average company and a great company.

At Barefoot, we called that "other stuff" hustle. We had to hustle, and everybody we hired had to as well. Our team was aware that the major advantage we had over the big-name competitors was that we were lighter, faster, and able to adjust quickly to take advantage of sudden changes in the marketplace, not to mention pop-up opportunities. We *needed* people who could make the most of that.

For instance, when we heard of a distributor who lost a big brand in our price point, we went to them the same day with a proposal to put our product in all the stores that had carried that other brand. Hustle meant money to us, and we built a national award-winning brand in spite of the size of our staff, the size of our competitors, and the size of our budget.

So—how, exactly, can *you* hire for hustle? Well, part of it is instinct. First impressions mean a lot, so trust your gut when interviewing someone new. Beyond gut calls, though, here are a few good ways to test hustle:

- **Give them homework.** During the interview, give job candidates a verbal run-down of the position, your company's challenges, and your expectations for the position. Then have the candidate send you a one-page summary on a deadline. This will tell you volumes.

- **Take a water break.** During interviews, we would sometimes ask candidates to go out and get us some waters. We would watch how they got up, opened the door, left the room, how long they were gone, and how they moved on their return. Were they deliberate, determined, and focused, or were they unstable, slow, and just shuffling along? (Also, did they think they were "too good" to get water?)

- **Grab a file.** Ask interviewees to get a report on the other side of the room. This is also a great opportunity to see how they execute a simple physical task, and how long it takes them.

- **Take a walk.** After the interview, we would often invite interviewees to take a walk with us around a nearby lake. We would take mental notes on their cadence, posture, and balance. We walked rather quickly, and observed if they could keep up. Their body language shouted volumes. Our experience told us that their approach to the job, with all its challenges and deadlines, would not be much different than how they used their body to perform simple physical tasks.

- **Look in their trunk.** This is a tactic we often used when interviewing prospective salespeople, who would need to use their cars and be organized. We'd walk the interviewee to their car, give them something to put in their trunk (for instance, some products to sample), and voila! A quick glimpse of the car's interior would tell us a lot about how organized that person was. We weren't performing a white-glove inspection, certainly—but a backseat or trunk littered with fast-food wrappers, for instance, did tend to send a message.

Be creative, and come up with your own hustle tests. Think about what attributes you most want your people to have, and devise a way to gauge whether or not interviewees possess them. Remember, your company will be most successful when each person thinks like an entrepreneur, but works well on a team. You can teach technical skills, but you can't teach hustle.

Chapter Three

Don't skimp on training

Many companies approach orientation like it's a formality. It has to be done, but no one wants to waste too much time on it. So, new employees are ushered in, given a quick tour of the office and a rundown of the benefits offered, and then they're expected to get right to work. It seems leaders assume that more detailed information on things like the company's processes and customers will simply be absorbed by new hires as they go along.

Well, we're here to tell you that this minimalist approach to training can have some counterproductive consequences, especially where judgment, relationships, and potential are involved. Yes, being thorough with training will take more time, energy, and maybe even money on the front end. But the long-term benefits of making sure your people know not just the "whats" but also the "whys" of their jobs will be worth it.

There's a line of thinking among many top companies today that training and ongoing development is too costly and that it's best not to spend resources training and developing an employee who may not be with the company for very long. But here's the thing: Professional development is an essential part of attracting and keeping the best talent. People want to stay with companies that care enough to invest in them, not just via their salaries, but by helping them develop the skills that will help them build their careers. If you're not providing this kind of training, rest assured, they *will* move to a company that provides it.

When you invest in your employees, they notice. And as a result, they invest more in your company. Here are our recommendations for putting together a comprehensive training program:

- **Give them the *really* grand tour.** Give all new hires a thorough education in your company. Make sure they understand how the money gets into their paychecks, who the customer is at every level (including distributors, store chains, individual consumers, etc.), and how the process works to provide those customers with goods and services. Tell them what other departments or employees specialize in and explain how each person fits into the big picture. The orientation period should extend beyond the initial meeting(s) and continue into the first year as new employees become increasingly familiar with your company and their roles within it.

- **Encourage questions.** Listen carefully to the questions your new employees ask—not just to the actual questions, but to the assumptions, logic, and even preconceived notions *behind* the questions. They often mask real deep-seated misunderstandings the employee may hold about the way things work. At Barefoot, we would often get questions that could have been answered by a simple yes or no. Instead, we sometimes spent 15 minutes or more unraveling misconceptions that could lead to future problems.

  The point is, when people don't get a clear answer to their question, or more importantly, the reasoning behind that question, they tend to make up a plausible explanation that seems logical to them. Then they act on it. If they do this over time with no apparent negative repercussions, it gives them "permission" to believe the assumption is true, and that's where the trouble begins. These misconceptions can be ingrained for years until one day, you're shocked by unexpected behavior that suddenly costs the company thousands!

For example, we were surprised when a seasoned production staff manager suggested that we save money by simplifying the colors of our shipping containers. We were using one unique color for every type of wine—so, for instance, Chardonnay was a different color from Pinot Noir, which was a different color from Cabernet Sauvignon and so on. Now, this manager was suggesting that we be more "efficient" and just have three colored cases: red for all reds, green for all whites, and pink for all blushes.

Turns out, the manager had never been told why we used uniquely colored cases for each wine type, and as a result, thought it was an unnecessary and somewhat frivolous oversight. In fact, the multiple-color system was suggested to us by a forklift operator who pointed out that it would reduce confusion and mistakes in deliveries from the warehouse. The point? Whenever your company is doing something unique, make sure your new hires don't "standardize" it away! (Even if it saves money or makes *their* jobs easier!)

- **Match them up with mentors.** When a new employee comes on board, try to match them up with a more experienced worker (preferably in the same department or division) who can advise, teach, challenge, and encourage him. Why? When rookies are taken under the wings of respected veterans, they learn more quickly, make fewer mistakes, and have tangible evidence that their employer cares about their success on a personal level. On the other hand, asking experienced employees to guide new hires shows these veterans that you notice and value their expertise. And overall, mentoring relationships guarantee that valuable institutional knowledge is passed on while knitting your team more closely together. It's a win-win!

At Barefoot, we found that this extensive, three-pronged approach to orientation produced people who consistently improved our organization, processes, and relationships. Because our staff had a comprehensive view of how our company worked, they regularly suggested new or better procedures, reorganization, and even entirely new jobs that we didn't know were necessary, but became pivotal to our success. They often came up with unsolicited solutions to challenges we faced in execution and communication. Our company culture benefited immensely from our people's understanding of what was really happening and why. It gave them the respect they needed for their co-workers, affiliates, and customers, resulting in solid and productive relations.

So, start giving your new hires a thorough orientation. Don't stop at the job description, but include your entire business model and how it works to give your customers the goods and services that make everyone's job possible. Remember, when the cement is wet, you can move it with a trowel, but when it gets hard, you'll need a jackhammer!

Chapter Four

Use performance-based compensation, and share the wealth

Allow us to be blunt: We don't think that set salaries are a great idea. When you have a compensation plan based on an hourly rate, you're paying for attendance, *not* production. Regardless of how much they do or don't accomplish, your employees will have an "I was there; pay me!" attitude...and can you blame them? Instead, our experience has shown us that performance-based compensation is better for everyone: you, your employees, and your company as a whole.

We created a pretty radical pay system at Barefoot for a simple reason: Barefoot was a small company that needed to sell large quantities of merchandise, and we couldn't afford unproductive people. So basically, we asked employees to bet on their own productivity. (Or as Michael told job applicants, he was asking people to bet on themselves.)

For salespeople specifically (and to a lesser extent, sales support people), we offered a small base salary and told new hires, "The more you sell, the more you make. There's no limit." And in order to ensure that our employees didn't ease off when they felt they were making "enough," we set up an increasing incentive, so each step—though harder—would be worth a lot more than the last.

Here's an example of how it worked: If someone sold, say, 100 cases in April 2000, and 100 cases in April 2001 (these numbers are unrealistically small for simplicity), their commission would be the same in both years. But if they sold 10 percent more—110 cases—they would get $1 for every case over that 100, or $10 more.

If they sold 20 percent more in April 2001—120 cases—they would get $2 per case for every case over 100. Not just $1 for cases 101-110 and $2 for cases 111-120; they would make $2 for each case, or $40 more. They didn't just get higher pay for additional growth, they got the boost for *all* the growth. It kept multiplying. So, 30 percent more—130 cases—would earn $3 times 30 cases, or $90, and on up. (And again, keep in mind that these numbers are unrealistically small!)

At various points, we were chastised by other businesspeople who felt that we were "overpaying" salespeople. This was partially due to the fact that several of our top salespeople made more than we, the owners, did! Yet when we looked at the numbers, we knew we were doing the right thing.

Our unorthodox compensation system didn't stop with our salespeople, either. Performance-based pay also applied to our sales support staff (i.e., everyone who *wasn't* a salesperson). In addition to their salaries, these employees received bonuses based on quarterly sales.

At first, many members of our sales support staff were skeptical. For example, one bookkeeper claimed that it wasn't fair to be paid a bonus based on quarterly sales because bookkeepers could not affect sales. Turns out, that claim wasn't entirely accurate. Here's what happened: Soon thereafter, one of our salespeople got a last-minute meeting with "Mr. Big," a supermarket chain buyer, at 8:00 a.m. the next morning. And because the bookkeeper in question knew that his bonus would be affected by the sale, he made sure that the salesperson had all the necessary reports by 7:00 a.m. Needless to say, our salesperson came back to the office with the purchase order.

Here's another example of how pay-for-performance motivated our sales support staff. One day, a gentleman walked into our reception area wearing an aloha shirt and Bermuda shorts. Although he appeared to be on vacation, this man was checking out our wine display and everything written on the walls. Our receptionist, who knew that her bonus was based on sales, proactively asked the visitor if he was a wine buyer. When the man shared that he was actually a *big* wine buyer for a 30-store chain in the Southwest, our receptionist immediately introduced him to our national sales manager. And because this wine buyer was relaxed, on vacation, and in discovery mode, he ended up putting Barefoot in all of his 30 stores! You can bet that our receptionist *really* savored that particular quarter's bonus.

Overall, performance-based pay really helped Barefoot to grow, and best of all, the increased pay was "found money" that cost us nothing. Plus, we reduced turnover, which is the #1 hidden cost of doing business. Think about it: When members of your team leave, you don't just lose those employees; you lose their hours of training, their institutional knowledge, their relationships outside the company, and in the case of salespeople, you can lose customers who are more loyal to your former employees than the product they represented. Plus, it can be costly to look for and train new candidates.

Basically, our compensation system meant that producers couldn't afford to leave, and non-producers couldn't afford to stay. Meanwhile, we constantly attracted new go-getters who were willing to bet on themselves.

And if you don't want to change your compensation plans, there are other great ways to pay for performance. One simple yet effective option that we used with great results at Barefoot is a 401(k) matching contribution program, in which we matched our employees' 401(k) contributions based on how the company had done the previous quarter. So, our employees knew that the better the company did the higher their 401(k) match would be. It was a great motivator, and in fact, it still is. According to a recent *MarketWatch* article, a Fidelity Investments poll found that 43 percent of employees would take a lower salary for a higher 401(k) match. The same survey showed that when given a choice between compensation packages, employees chose lower salaries with higher matching contributions.[1]

It's simple: How you treat your employees directly correlates to how successful your business will be. If you treat them like a commodity—if you're stingy with pay, recognition, and benefits—they'll do only the bare minimum to keep their jobs, and eventually, they'll leave.

We suggest you use performance-based compensation, too. Yes, every company and every industry is different, but if it's possible to earn profits, it's possible to tie those profits to your employees' salaries and bonuses—and we guarantee that you'll see results! Sharing the wealth never looked so good!

---

[1] Andrea Coombes, "Bigger 401(k) match trumps bigger salary," *MarketWatch*, 12 August 2014, accessed 14 August 2014, http://www.marketwatch. com/story/bigger-401k-match-trumps-bigger-salary-2014-08-12.

Chapter Five

Get out of your employees' way

Increasing productivity is a prime goal for today's companies. They want to get more done, more quickly and efficiently. When your company isn't able to meet its goals, your first inclination might be to blame your employees for being unable to execute. But we would caution you to take a look in the mirror before doling out blame.

That's because often leaders who want to blame their employees for not executing are actually using a leadership style that is keeping people from getting things done.

Read on to see if you fall under any of these leadership types and consider what you can do to get out of your employees' way so that they can execute at a higher level:

- **The Solo Artist.** You've worked hard to earn the leadership role you have now, and you're not about to do anything that could jeopardize it. So rather than seek out your team's thoughts and opinions or delegate projects to them, you keep everything on your plate. You don't pass on your team's bright ideas. You control the information that reaches them so that they have to go through you to get to other leaders or departments. The result is you're stifling your employees' upward movement, and you're probably creating resentment in the ranks. Not to mention that you're causing the company to miss out on being able to take advantage of their ideas and expertise. Most likely, your employees think you don't trust them and that your style of leadership is going to prevent them from being able to advance. Keep it up and you'll only alienate them more, possibly to the point of them wanting to leave your company.

- **The Bottleneck.** Your employees do what you ask them to do. They do it well, and they do it on time. The problem is, you refuse to let their work see the light of day until you've personally reviewed it. Now, everything from proposals to reports to marketing plans are piling up on your desk faster than you can read them. Employees are left twiddling their thumbs as they wait for your feedback. No one feels comfortable making a decision without your approval, which might be days in coming. Sure, your company is hitting its goals, but not nearly as quickly as it might if you loosened the reins.

- **The Compliance Stalwart.** Consider this possibly familiar scenario: An employee comes up with a great idea, but before he or she can really explore it, you insist it go through compliance. Of course, smart leaders should always look out for their company's best interests and keeping compliance top of mind is one way to do that. Still, does *everything* need to go through compliance? If yes, then consider whether the wait for compliance approval is so long that your people get discouraged or frustrated to the point of not wanting to share future ideas. If no, take a moment to think about why you're insisting the company's compliance attorneys approve every new idea. Are you just overly cautious? Are you afraid of the change the new idea could bring around? Or are you wary of sticking your neck out for your employees and saying, "This is a really great idea"? Regardless, if you want a true entrepreneurial culture, you must find a way to put your attorneys on a shorter leash.

- **The Client/Customer Hoarder.** Maybe you have no problem delegating the easy stuff that has to get done like meeting talking points, project memos, etc. But when it comes to letting employees lead client presentations or go after new accounts on their own, you just can't seem to turn over the reins. Or you seem to turn them over but then butt in on every client/employee email you're CCed on. You spend large chunks of your time answering client questions and performing tasks per their request that other employees could do just as well, and as a result, you neglect the things that you, and only you, can handle.

- **The Helicopter.** You congratulate yourself on letting your employees do their own thing. You're confident that you've delegated the right tasks to the right people. Problem is, you watch your employees complete those tasks from start to finish. You're constantly hovering around your team's workspace observing, correcting, asking questions, and interfering. "Micromanager" might as well be your job title.

Be honest. Do you engage in any of these behaviors? If so, it's important to stop, step back, and show your people that you trust them to make important decisions and do important work. When you do, you'll give your team the freedom they need to help move the company forward—and you'll free up a lot of time and energy for yourself, too.

But wait, you say. When they're not under my direct scrutiny, won't my people make some mistakes from time to time? Sure. They might make errors you would have caught, or they might forget to cover all the pertinent details. However, if you encourage them to make mistakes the right way, they will improve the company's procedures and training manuals in the process.

If you have trouble stepping back, ask yourself: *How legitimate are my concerns? Has the employee/team in question given me a reason to doubt their capabilities, or am I letting "what ifs" and fears get the best of me?* As long as the answer is the latter, take a deep breath, step back, and let your employees do their jobs. Remind yourself that your company hires capable, motivated people (and if that's not the case, move them out of your organization!) and that if anyone does run into a challenge, they know where to find you.

Chapter Six

Delegate effectively

Delegation is tricky for even some of the best leaders. And it's usually not because of the reasons you might think. We often have a picture in our minds of the harried, multi-tasking leader who just refuses to relinquish control of any of his tasks or projects to one of his subordinates. But often, it isn't about control at all. Often, leaders want to delegate, but they don't want it to look like they're just dumping unwanted tasks on their employees, or they don't feel they have the time needed to train an employee to do a task.

What all leaders should know is that delegation plays an essential role in providing your employees with ongoing training. It's how you build your bench. When one of your employees can take over a project team or start running a weekly meeting, it frees you up to take care of bigger issues, and it provides them with an opportunity to advance and strengthen their role inside your company.

But like many tasks, delegation is easier said than done.

Here's the first step to take when it comes to delegation: Start handing over those tasks and projects that your employees can do or can *almost* do without your input. Trust their expertise and trust that if they really hit a wall, they'll come to you.

Here are some additional principles to keep in mind.

- **Match the assignment to the employee.** One very important thing to keep in mind is that delegation isn't just about handing out tasks to your team. It's about matching the right job to the right person, and using your assets effectively. The fact is, everybody excels at something. Everyone has a unique set of skills, abilities, and talents. Even two people with the same job description might have significantly different strengths and interests! Your responsibility is to look at all of the things that need to happen in your company and make sure the right people are put in those positions.

- **Create new jobs if you have to!** Sometimes an employee's skill set won't exactly match a pre-existing job description. When that happens, create a new position! Give employees the tasks they are uniquely equipped to handle, and delegate the rest of their former job descriptions to others. In other words, don't put the square peg in the round hole. Build a square hole. You might be surprised by the positive response from everyone in your organization.

- **Delegate for growth.** This is something of a balancing act: You want to give your people tasks they're capable of carrying out; however, you should also try to "stretch" them so that they are constantly learning, growing, and expanding their skill sets—not to mention propelling your company forward! For example, give your salespeople progressively bigger accounts. Ask your marketing team to develop a campaign that expands your brand's reach to a new demographic this quarter. At Barefoot, we provided bonuses not just for volume, but for growth. As a new company we knew that there was no treading water. We had to swim upstream or be washed downstream.

- **Let your employees help.** Ultimately, the task of delegation is up to you. But that doesn't mean you can't ask for your employees' input. Often, your people will have firm—and sometimes surprising!—ideas about what they'd like to take on. And from an employee engagement standpoint, it's always a good idea to make sure your people know their preferences have been heard and taken into account.

At Barefoot, we kept job descriptions very fluid. We knew that in order for us to stay relevant in the midst of changing times while still delivering stellar customer service, many job descriptions would become obsolete within a year. So every year, we asked our people to rewrite their job descriptions, encouraging them to tell us what aspects of their jobs they felt uncomfortable performing. We would then offer up those tasks to the whole team. Almost invariably, we were surprised to discover that every task was picked up by someone who actually wanted to do it. Based on this redistribution of tasks, we'd revise everyone's job descriptions yet again...at least until the next year! In the meantime, all of our employees took impressive ownership of their jobs because they had a hand in designing them.

We'll never forget one new hire named Debbie who initially worked the front desk. At the end of her first year, we told Debbie she was doing great and asked what else she would like to try. She responded, "How about Accounts Receivable?" We were surprised because this was the department that collected money owed to Barefoot, sometimes by people who, let's be honest, preferred to stall.

"Really?" Michael asked. "That's the most frustrating job in the company."

"My mom and dad owned an insurance company," Debbie replied. "I understand the problems. I think I can help."

And you know what? Debbie was right. Her insight, along with the fact that she was hyper-organized, understood people, and was charming, allowed her to excel in her new position. Within months, accounts receivable was humming, and pretty much everyone who owed money seemed unusually good about paying up. We're so glad we allowed Debbie to have a say in which tasks she felt she excelled at!

Finally, avoid micromanaging at all costs. Give supervision, advice, and guidance, certainly—but don't babysit. If you've put proper thought into delegation, your people will be able to handle the tasks you've given them—and they'll do their best work knowing that you have confidence in their abilities.

Chapter Seven

Let information flow freely

Some companies make the mistake of treating information like a coveted commodity. In fact, it's often used as a type of currency—the right juicy piece of info can buy you lunch, help get you a promotion, bring kudos your way, or be traded for other valuable information. And then, some information is downright suppressed because it may threaten some supervisor's concept of job security.

The flipside of this, of course, is that in large siloed organizations it's completely normal for one department or division to have no clue what the others are up to. No department is actively keeping information from any other. The information simply isn't flowing because no one is communicating. *We each have totally different functions to perform,* the thinking goes, *so there's no need to waste time comparing notes and sharing updates.* Can you see how that attitude might cause problems?

You probably won't be surprised to hear that we are vehemently opposed to a "need-to-know" policy when it comes to information.

Instead, we advocate a "know-the-need" approach. Why? As we have said many times before, your people are your greatest assets. They are full of intelligence, ideas, and passion—you just have to unlock those things! So do whatever you can to engage your entire team and keep the information free-flowing.

Here's how we made know-the-need work at Barefoot. You've already encountered some of these ideas in previous chapters, but we'll review them here because they're all crucial to the dissemination of information:

- **Be transparent about everything, warts and all.** When you have good news, it's easy to be transparent with your employees. ("Get excited—last quarter's sales campaign was 20 percent more successful than we'd hoped!") However, you may be tempted to keep bad news and problems to yourself. Don't. Be honest about the challenges your company is facing, and ask the entire staff for solutions. You'll probably get them! In large part, that's because—as author John Kotter says—transparency is key to creating urgency. Without it, people will sink into a dangerous complacency.[1]

  When you think about them, Kotter's teachings make perfect sense. If your people realize that your business is dangerously close to being in the red, for example, or that a new competitor is aggressively grabbing up the market share (and what these developments mean for their own salaries!), they will naturally be more motivated to act. If you *don't* share the concerning news, though, of course your people can't be expected to do anything about it.

  At Barefoot, we often invited the entire office staff to brainstorming sessions. We would tell everyone about whatever problem or challenge we were facing at the time, and then open the floor up for discussion. It wasn't unusual to hear some off-the-wall, cockamamie ideas—especially at first—but those crazy suggestions had a way of triggering other ideas from other people, and eventually leading to a wonderful solution.

For instance, at one meeting we shared with our team that we had just lost a distributor in another state—a distributor who had been supplying numerous retailers with our products. If there was any lapse in supply, Barefoot would almost surely be discontinued by those retailers. One person suggested that we try to deliver our product directly, which turned out to be illegal in the state in question. A second person asked if another distributor could step in, but there were only a couple of choices, and none of them seemed feasible.

Then someone wondered aloud if any other wine brands had recently lost or "fired" their distributors. Now we were on to something! Soon, we discovered a big distributor who had just lost a major brand at our price point. We immediately approached that distributor with our existing business and also suggested that the distributor use Barefoot in place of the brand they had just lost.

In this way, we not only solved the immediate problem, but we increased our business. In fact, as Barefoot grew, we kept looking for bigger distributors who had lost big brands at our price point. This became a signature distribution strategy to improve our service to retailers and grow our brand.

- **Help employees interpret the information you give them.**
  One problem that often crops up within transparent organizations is that there's *so much* data flowing that it's overwhelming. Your employees might need you to direct their focus toward what's most important, connect the dots, and explain things they might not understand. For instance, you might need to say, "Pay attention to this number. It means our standing in the marketplace has fallen from X (where

it was last year) to Y. To get back to where we need to be, we'll have to improve next quarter's sales by 15 percent." Remember, it doesn't matter how much data is available if your employees aren't able to understand or interpret it in a way that drives action.

At Barefoot, we always broke data down into simple, actionable goals. For instance, we would tell our staff that the company's ability to match their 401(k) contributions was directly related to our quarterly profits. The more money the company made, the higher the match. Then we would identify the sales and cost factors that influenced those profits. Needless to say, our people strove to earn the highest 401(k) match from our company!

- **Link compensation to overall performance.** When everyone's paychecks and bonuses are linked to overall sales, your employees will have a big incentive to share information and ideas to keep the company moving forward.

We always made it very clear to our people that if they weren't in sales, they were in sales support—no matter what their job titles were. And to make that point, everyone's bonuses were based on sales and profitability. Because their incomes depended on it, people regularly came up with cost-saving ideas and methods to increase sales, even when they worked in seemingly unrelated jobs such as reception, accounting, or the warehouse.

For instance, our warehouse people once devised a way to save money on the cost of printed marketing materials. They discovered that most of these expensive materials never made it to the retail shelf and were in fact thrown away by our distributors. So they began creating neatly organized packets containing the small cards and signs needed for each retail display. Then, our warehouse workers made sure that the packets were sent directly to our account representatives, rather than to the distributors' warehouses. We saved tens of thousands of dollars every year once our marketing materials made it directly into the hands of the people responsible for putting them on the shelves!

- **Give employees a detailed understanding of how your company works.** It's important to realize that unless your employees have a detailed knowledge of your company (how each part relates to all the others—and most importantly, how money travels through the organization and into their paychecks), being transparent won't be much good.

We would regularly sit Barefoot's employees down and take them through the "money trail" that led to their pay, bonuses, and benefits. If someone asked a question or took some action that demonstrated a misconception about how our finances "worked," we would immediately stop to correct that misunderstanding. We'd go over the money trail again and again until the employee understood how their actions affected their compensation. Only then were we able to proceed with the confidence that our people would make the right decisions going forward.

- **Invite everyone to sales meetings.** Since everyone in your company is either sales or sales support, it makes sense to run everything by your salespeople that affects your product and its image. Before you allow a change or "improvement" to the product or the package, check with the folks who have to actually make the sale, overcome the objections, and talk directly to the decision makers and the end users. When it comes to products, package design, and even marketing, top-down thinking can undermine what has taken years to establish. Make sure the people on the front lines (the salespeople) have given you their input before any "improvements" are made.

Furthermore, sharing information at company-wide sales meetings means that more people will have the opportunity to share their skills. For example, when Barefoot had sales meetings, everyone was invited, all the way to the people in Accounting. To the accountants, sales was an exciting world. They'd get energized. They'd throw out ideas, ask if more comparisons and better-detailed numbers would help the sales crew.

"Sure," the salespeople would say.

"We'll get you those every Monday," the accountants would announce, suddenly more jazzed about their jobs and proud that they could contribute.

And, of course, inviting everyone to sales meetings gives salespeople themselves the opportunity to ask other departments for what they need. At one such meeting, our salespeople complained that our small sales signs were mysteriously disappearing off retail shelves. (We suspected that over-zealous representatives from the competition were the culprits.) Our salespeople asked if there was some way to put signs directly on the bottles so that they would always get to the shelf, and would be harder to lose or remove.

"Sure," our production people said. They designed signs that hung around the necks of the bottles, ensuring that the signs always got to the shelf. We eventually took this concept even further and put stickers depicting the medals we had won right on the bottle glass itself. All this happened because production heard what sales had to say, and knew that their own compensation was tied to sales.

- **Reward good ideas.** Always reward good ideas and acknowledge a job well done. If your people don't feel that their efforts are noticed and appreciated, they won't have a compelling reason to act on new information, no matter how freely it flows through your organization!

Keep in mind that one of the most appreciated rewards is public acknowledgment, in front of your whole organization. At Barefoot, our lawyers advised against this practice because if a publicly-praised employee got fired, they could sue for wrongful termination. (After all, they'd have documentation proving that they were appreciated!) The problem with this fear-driven mentality is that it actually *causes* turnover because employees feel that they are taken for granted.

So against our lawyers' advice, we did, in fact, single out employees who improved production, reduced costs, improved customer service, or improved sales. We made it clear that their contribution affected everybody's income. When the rest of our employees got these memos, they received two important messages. First, "If I do this, I will be recognized too," and second, "Now I have a better understanding of what this person does, and how they affect my job and my income."

- **Don't limit free speech.** What we mean is, make sure that your company's culture is one of safety and mutual respect. Of course your employees shouldn't be able to bash a co-worker with impunity, for instance, but they *should* feel free to speak their minds about relevant issues, even if they aren't delivering positive news or agreeing with your assessment of a situation. Think about it: If an employee sees a potential hole in your marketing plan or has a sales pitch that conflicts with yours, you *want* that person to speak up! And you also want your people to feel comfortable admitting to mistakes. When people withhold information because they're fearful of your (or any other leader's) reaction, you're hamstringing your organization.

[1.] John Kotter, "How Can Leaders Root Out Complacency from Their Organization?" *Forbes*, 16 May 2012, accessed 13 August 2014, http://www.forbes.com/sites/johnkotter/2012/05/16/how-can-leaders-root-out-complacency-from-their-organization/.

Chapter Eight

Don't wait for perfectly sunny conditions to allow employees to take the initiative on a project

Let's face it: In a topsy-turvy market, when everyone at companies from the top to the bottom is slammed from the time they walk through the door until they leave for the day, no one wants to rock the boat too much. As a result, good ideas get put to the side.

But that move can be very costly. When your employees watch you uphold the status quo, they'll tend to do so as well. As a result, they'll stop bringing out good ideas. And when that happens, innovation—one of the essential methods for gaining a competitive advantage in today's economy—freezes at your company.

So, to create a culture where entrepreneurial thinking can thrive, you must make sure everyone understands that great ideas are always welcome. Then, give your employees the freedom to move forward on projects, even when conditions aren't exactly sunny.

The truth is, if we had let our "we'll be ready whens" dictate our business decisions, we'd probably still be wannabe winemakers. When we launched Barefoot Cellars, all we had was a laundry room to use as an office, a bank account that was running on fumes, and no knowledge of our industry. And yet we gave ourselves the freedom to take the leap. We knew the risks, but we believed in what we were doing, so we went for it.

You have to give your employees the same benefit.

Looking back, we firmly believe that our lack of, well, *everything* (capital, experience, preparation, and planning, just to name a few) was the key to our success. Some of Barefoot's greatest innovations came about because our company was caught in a downpour and we needed to patch some holes in the roof, *fast*. Sound familiar?

The lesson here is a simple one: Conditions will never be perfect for any idea or initiative. Instead, you need to settle for "mostly sunny with a chance of showers" (or even "light drizzle"), and plan to get a little wet. Keep in mind that if your employees don't ever feel comfortable enough to share these ideas or launch these projects, your company will *definitely* never benefit from them.

There may be some hiccups, sure. But it's better to give your employees the freedom to create than to never allow them to start at all. It's more productive to roll with the punches than it is to avoid them altogether. And as our experience has taught us, until you start doing the actual work, there are some things you simply *can't* prepare for. We learned some of our most valuable lessons through doing, whether the *doing* led to success or an informative mistake, not through reading or studying. And we're betting the same will be true for your employees.

So—the next time an employee approaches you with a new promotional idea or wants to shake up how your company's departments are organized, give them the reins. Don't let less than perfect conditions hold your employees back from acting now.

Chapter Nine

Ask a lot of questions

At a time when creative problem solving and innovation are a must-have at every company, it's important for C-Suiters to remember this important fact: The best person to handle a problem at your company isn't you; it's the person closest to the problem—no matter where that person falls on the totem pole.

But are your employees equipped with the information they need to solve problems creatively and efficiently? If they ask upper-management a question about why certain processes have been put in place, will they get an answer?

You have to make sure the answer to *that* question is always YES! The more your employees understand about why your company uses certain processes, the more likely they'll be able to solve problems when they arise—often a lot more quickly and for less money than if a solution has to come from on high.

Opening your door to employee questions is a great way to infuse entrepreneurial thinking into your employees' work, and frankly, it's the best way to make improvements to company operations. We know because asking questions in order to solve problems was how we were able to make Barefoot Wine a success.

We've already told you that when we got into the wine industry we knew next to nothing about it. And because we were starting from scratch, we found ourselves needing to answer questions that would have never occurred to most industry professionals. In fact, many of our knowledge gaps were so basic that most people in the industry had stopped thinking about them: *Which demographic buys the most wine? Which price is the most popular? How do you sell it? How does this work?*

Our ignorance ended up being an asset. To get the knowledge we needed, we had to pick the brains of people at every level of the industry, from winery owners to grape pickers to supermarket managers and wine distributors. In fact, we purposefully made friends with people from whom most producers never ask for input (like forklift operators and bottling machine operators) because we knew they could give us practical, on-the-street advice.

The answers we received from folks who had "been there, done that" ended up being more valuable than any business course we could have taken. For instance, we'll never forget Michael's encounter with one supermarket chain's gruff wine buyer. Michael asked what our logo should look like, and got this answer:

"You know, Houlihan, nobody ever asked me that before, so I'm gonna help you. Don't make it a hill or a leap or a run or a valley or a creek...Don't put a flower on it. And for crissakes, don't make it a chateau! Make the logo the same as the name...And whatever you do, put it in plain English...And, Houlihan, make it visible from four feet away. She [the shopper] has to be able to see it when she's pushing her cart down the aisle. Now get outta here. I got work to do."

Turns out, that advice was solid gold, and we didn't have to pay a dime for it. All we had to do was ask a question.

So, here's our advice to you: Encourage your employees to ask questions. The payoff? They'll be more knowledgeable about how the company works and therefore more capable of solving problems and making improvements. They might even discover some game-changing insights that your competitors have overlooked. And all because you answered a few questions.

Chapter Ten

Never waste a perfectly good mistake

Most leaders look at mistakes as something to be avoided, and as a result, they pass that sentiment down to their employees. But the most innovative, agile companies embrace mistakes. When you move from a culture that punishes mistakes to one that embraces them, your employees will have the freedom to take risks, and that's where entrepreneurial thinking leads to great innovation.

Of course, not every mistake that happens will lead to a great innovation. But we think you'll find that most of them will lead to an improvement. When an employee makes a mistake, you want a culture that encourages him or her to learn from the mistake and change what led to it rather than a culture that encourages him to fear punishment and sweep that mistake under the rug. Cultures where mistakes are embraced are cultures where there is more transparency. They acknowledge mistakes, the respective parties take responsibility for them and learn from them, and then everyone moves forward.

As you might imagine, *many* mistakes were made as we grew Barefoot Cellars—by us, sometimes by our employees, and sometimes by others. As such, we developed a fairly robust standard operating procedure. Overall, we lived by the idea that blame is disempowering, but taking responsibility for the future is empowering to everyone. Here are the highlights from our mistake playbook—tips that are important for you and your employees. They helped us not only survive, but thrive—and they can do the same for you.

- **Cop to it.** The sooner you admit to the error, the more you reduce the drama…and the faster you can move on to the next, more important stage: What you are going to do about the situation. Plus, admitting to imperfection demonstrates a level of transparency, authenticity, vulnerability, and humanity that can actually gain others' respect and loyalty.

- **Recognize how it happened.** It's very important to investigate how and why an error occurred so that you can fix the faulty procedure or process. That's why Barefoot made sure employees weren't afraid to make or report mistakes (those involving technical errors, that is—we were adamant that bad behavior or an inability to perform should not be overlooked). We cultivated a "culture of permission" that encouraged employees to look at mistakes creatively and share their solutions.

  Basically, our approach to mistakes was to say, "Congratulations! You found a new way to screw up, and that's a good thing. We didn't know that this could happen, but now that it has, we can keep it from happening again." Honestly, we think that large siloed organizations where you can be demoted, passed over, or even fired for a mistake are missing the boat. That's because real progress in progressive companies is often built on the backs of mistakes and the improvements they spark.

- **Aim, don't blame.** Once you've figured out why a mistake happened, resolve to stop playing the *blame* game. Instead, encourage your employees to *aim* their focus on what they can do to prevent the situation from reoccurring. This lesson was driven home to us during one of Michael's business trips to Chicago. He was supposed to show some new wines to retailers, and the samples had been shipped to his hotel.

However, when the package arrived, the hotel didn't check to see that Michael was on the reservation list—they only noticed that he wasn't currently occupying a room—and they sent the package back. Technically, Michael's lack of samples wasn't our fault, because the hotel didn't do their due diligence. But to our buyers, all that mattered was that the new wines weren't there.

From that point on, we at Barefoot worked to make sure that no package would ever be refused in error again. After some trial and error, every box of wine was ultimately decorated on all six sides with instructions to the hotel *not* to return the box, and details of when Michael would be arriving. We also included Barefoot's contact information and instructed the reader to get in touch with the hotel manager, whom we had told to expect the package, before sending it back. Overkill? Not really. Because the problem was solved.

- **Make mistakes W-R-I-T-E.** It's crucial for your employees to take the lessons they learn and physically make them part of the company's policies. When your employees make a mistake, encourage them to consider whether a new procedure, checklist, or sign-off sheet is needed. Ask them to bring you their solution for how the mistake can be turned into a written permanent improvement for the company.

Don't waste time and energy beating well-meaning employees up when mistakes are made. Instead, use these golden opportunities to improve the way your company operates.

Chapter Eleven

The ball is always in your court

Here's one thing that all successful business leaders have in common: They learn to eat problems for breakfast. It's a survival necessity. When you're leading a business, there is an unending onslaught of daily challenges. As soon as one issue or problem is solved, another one pops up, whack-a-mole style.

As a successful business leader, you understand something essential: *The ball is always in your court.* And that's a lesson you have to teach your employees. Make sure they understand that it's up to them to find a way forward, even if (*especially* if!) an answer isn't immediately obvious. Remind them that because they're the ones closest to certain problems, they're best equipped to solve them.

We certainly don't have all the problem-solving answers, but we do have a proven formula for successfully staying afloat. Here are six problem-solving tips for you to share with your employees:

- **Accept responsibility.** You have to take responsibility for all outcomes. If you allow yourself to believe that the ball is in someone else's court, you're on the way to losing momentum and control. So what does taking responsibility look like in the real world?

It might mean doing the other guy's job without offending him. In other words, when you're in the heat of the moment, don't wait around for someone else to take action. Do what you have to do to move things forward. Afterward, work with the person who may have been the holdup to create a process that will allow things to run more smoothly in the future.

Or it might mean focusing on a solution instead of looking around to assign blame. When you blame, you disempower yourself and become a victim. We say, "Aim; don't blame." In other words, aim your focus at yourself. Ask yourself how you can clean up your own backyard.

For instance, at one point, we kept getting bottling contracts that said that our wines would be bottled according to standard winemaking procedures, but we couldn't find a list of these procedures anywhere. No one we asked in the industry could give us a list of "standard" winemaking procedures. But of course, we wanted to ensure our wines always met the Barefoot standard for quality. So we sat down with our winemaker, wrote down a set of procedures, and added them to our bottling contracts as specifications that had to be met before we would pay for bottling.

For us, accepting responsibility meant creating our own bottling standards. For you, it might mean adding a new checklist item or a whole new procedure to help you to get around a roadblock, misunderstanding, or mistake in the future. Whatever the circumstances, do what you can to make a successful outcome more likely.

- **Chill out, and expect to see solutions.** Don't allow yourself to wallow in nerve-wracking what-ifs. Don't waste time wringing your hands. Getting anxious and freaked out can actually make you less effective! You need a calm demeanor to allow your eyes and ears to communicate with your brain and give it some time to think about the problem from all angles. And after taking a few deep breaths, tell yourself (sternly and repeatedly, if need be!) that solutions and opportunities are ahead.

Once, we thought we had an unwinnable legal battle on our hands. A giant European company was copying our label and told us that even though we had the EU trademark, we could not afford to sustain a three-year lawsuit. (They were right!) After a lot of panic, we finally calmed down and realized that we did not have to fight this company in the legal arena, where they had us out-gunned with teams of lawyers and a giant war chest. It dawned on us that the big buyers would not want confusion in their stores. And, we realized, those buyers would want to be on the side of the brand with the legal rights to the name and logo. Bypassing the legal system altogether and going to the source of this company's income forced them to back down. Thank goodness we forced ourselves to take a few calming deep breaths before getting the lawyers involved!

- **Back up and take inventory.** When you're facing a problem, it will benefit you to back up and take the 10,000-foot view. Pretend that you're an outsider learning about your position and your company for the first time. Go over all of your assets: colleagues, leaders, clients, industry peers, etc. You may be surprised to re-identify assets that you've been overlooking, or advantages you've been ignoring, which could help you troubleshoot a current problem.

At Barefoot, we suddenly got an opportunity to expand our brand into a very large Florida supermarket chain, but we couldn't afford to purchase the materials we'd need to service the customer. After freaking out for a few days, we realized that our glass supplier would benefit greatly from this expansion, as would our label printer and several other suppliers. Because we maintained an excellent relationship with them and kept them abreast of our successes and shortcomings, they trusted us. So when we asked these partners to "invest" their materials in their own future expansion, they gave us extended credit to cover the order.

- **Get into puzzle-solving mode.** Many times the solution is a simple one that solves more than one problem. So get all your other problems out there on the table as well. Pretend that they're all pieces of one giant puzzle. Look at them from different angles and see how they might relate to one another.

  For instance, we once had a problem getting a distributor to carry our product in Alabama. None of the big distributors would even talk to us! But then we heard that a major competing brand was pulling out of one of the top distributors in that state. We convinced that distributor to seamlessly replace the brand they had lost with Barefoot. Our problem solved their problem!

- **Find allies.** Who else is affected by the problem and stands to gain by its solution? Who else succeeds when you succeed? Identify these possible allies, then discuss your problems with them. Often, other entities will be willing to make accommodations on your behalf when they see how they themselves will benefit.

  Once, we were having trouble getting into Wisconsin chain stores. But we *did* find a retailer in Wisconsin who had five stores. Because we gave this retailer an exclusive on our brand for five years, he not only promoted it, but the sales in his five stores were greater than the sales we could have expected in the major Wisconsin supermarkets! He stood to gain by an exclusive on a hot seller that was *not* in the chain stores.

- **Let it simmer.** Sometimes, the best solutions pop up when you least expect them. Even when you are not actively searching for a solution, "the little grey cells," as Agatha Christie's famous detective Hercule Poirot says, "are working all the time; they see everything." So give them a lot to look at. Put your best efforts toward overcoming the challenge. If you aren't immediately successful, give your brain a break, get away from it all, and let it simmer. Often, when you do this, the solution finds you.

At Barefoot, we were able to find a way to get several upscale wine shops that wouldn't carry Barefoot to start carrying it. The problem was that these shops viewed Barefoot as "just ordinary wine." Their wines were expensive, vintage-dated, vineyard-designated wines for their wine-knowledgeable and affluent clientele. However, when those same clients needed to buy wines for their daughters' weddings, they would take their money elsewhere and spend it on large magnums of less expensive wine, usually from a supermarket or a big box store. When we were able to demonstrate to the wine shops that this was happening, we were able to solve our problem of getting into the shops by solving their problem of not offering their upscale customers magnums of value wine. They kept the money in their shops, and we got the sale!

Chapter Twelve

Make sure you're solving the right problems

L ike you, your employees often have to spend their days jumping from one task to the next at a mile-a-minute speed. And when that's the case, it's all too easy for them to make the mistake of not paying enough attention to all the possible repercussions of the decisions they make. In fact, the "ready, fire, aim" approach to decision making they adopt in order to check items off their to-do lists usually only leads to *more* problems and *more* time spent trying to fix them.

The end result? Those problems get kicked up to you. And often, at that point, they're bigger and even more difficult to solve. That's why it's so important for your employees to learn how to anticipate problems and solve the *right* ones.

If we hadn't learned this invaluable skill set, Barefoot would simply refer to the state of being shoeless, not a bestselling wine brand! Here's a list of our greatest problem-anticipating hits (some will sound familiar!):

- **Look before you leap.** Many problems encountered during the course of your employees' days could have been prevented if they had taken a moment to consider possible consequences before making their move. There *is* a happy medium between being proactive and being cautious.

  Since they don't have a crystal ball, the best way for your employees to look before they leap is to ask themselves questions about all aspects of the company and their roles within it, with an eye to anticipating problems. Being aware of what could go wrong in these areas will keep them from being taken by surprise. It will also give them a head start in formulating a response plan if certain scenarios do occur.

- **Make sure you understand what the real issue is.** If they don't know what the issue is, they may end up seeking solutions for something that isn't even a problem. They may even end up making the problem worse.

  To use a simple example, say that a new marketing campaign isn't getting the results your head of marketing wants. Assuming that she's not reaching enough people, she throws the remaining bits of her marketing budget at buying more ad space online. But as it turns out, the problem isn't that the audience isn't big enough—the problem is that the sports-themed ads simply don't appeal to enough people. Her desperate expenditure won't boost the company, because she's "solved" the wrong problem.

- **Perform a weekly problem analysis.** What's coming up in the week ahead? Client meetings? New product rollout? Any colleagues on vacation? Before each week, encourage your employees to take some time to think about what's on the books for the week ahead. They should consider what problems might pop up and what they'll do if they do, so that they aren't needlessly blindsided. Being prepared really is half the battle.

- **Make sure you patch all the holes.** Often, when a problem pops up, your employees fix it and forget it. After all, their plates are full—they need to move on to the next thing as quickly as possible! Of course, the downside of this approach is that nothing is done to keep the problem from happening again. At Barefoot, we operated under the principle most clearly defined by our National Sales Manager Randy Arnold: Never Waste a Perfectly Good Mistake.

  We brainstormed every mistake, even small ones. Those sessions weren't about who was to blame, but what went wrong—what communications failed, what was overlooked, what was ambiguous, what Barefoot didn't know. And then we created procedures and lists so Barefoot could do everything possible to try to keep that problem from happening again.

- **Make sure the right people are talking to each other.** How many times have you heard, "Well, I thought so-and-so was going to take care of that." Or, "I missed the deadline because no one told me it had been moved up." Or, "I didn't realize the client wasn't satisfied with that part of the strategy."

  These miscommunications are problems in and of themselves, but they're even bigger problems waiting to happen. Often, big mess-ups can be avoided by simply checking that the lines of communication are open and operating well at your company. The best way to promote transparency? Don't build a need-to-know culture—build a know-the-need culture.

- **Train employees to be problem scouts.** Encourage employees to be on the lookout for possible problems, and reward them when they come up with solutions. At Barefoot, we found that making sure each employee understood the company's cash flow (aka, where their paychecks came from!) really encouraged this type of entrepreneurial thinking.

- **Put yourself in the other person's shoes.** No matter the situation, ask yourself these questions: What might the other person (customer, vendor, colleague, etc.) be thinking? What do they expect from me? What might they misunderstand without an explanation from me? Putting yourself in the other person's shoes can keep you on track and prevent you from making a lot of mistakes.

- **Understand that your customers' problems are your problems too.** When your employees *really* understand your customers' world, they can serve them at a deeper level. This way your company becomes a trusted advisor instead of "just" a vendor.

When we first started Barefoot, we were operating under the misconception that folks in the distribution channel had a financial interest in keeping our product in stock. Boy, were we wrong! The biggest issue we faced turned out to be our product being out-of-stock, *not* sales. It took us a little while to understand that our distributors had hundreds of products besides ours that were paying their bills. Remembering to restock Barefoot (a wine that was new and unproven) when it was sold out was a challenge for them.

That wasn't the extent of the issue, though. Retailers depended on the distributors' representatives to tell them when they were out of stock. So if retailers didn't get the prompt from our distributors' representatives, they would allow their stock of Barefoot to run out and even become discontinued. Ultimately, we had to have our own representative go into most of the stores and get the reorders for the distributors' representatives.

The point? Distributors' and retailers' overloaded books and shelves full of products became our problem too. If we had not stepped up to do what we had originally thought was *their* job, we would have never gotten a reorder from the distributor, and Barefoot would not be here today!

Employing all of these strategies is like keeping your knees bent in tennis. When you're standing rigidly (i.e., not considering what-ifs and not being proactive) it's difficult to get yourself into position to hit the ball—unless, of course, it goes exactly where you wanted it to. (And how often does that happen?!?) But a knees-bent stance (i.e., trying to anticipate problems) makes your employees more agile and responsive. Their likelihood of getting to the ball, no matter where it lands on the court, goes up.

Chapter Thirteen

Learn to extrapolate

Business is more complex than ever and because of that, companies can't possibly train their employees for every possible scenario. It isn't a doable or a viable way to run a company. That's why you must prepare your employees to extrapolate—to use what they've learned elsewhere to improve and build on the work they do for your company.

Unfortunately, extrapolation is actually a dying art. We think it's one of the unintended side effects of living in such an information-rich society. In an age when you can find the answer to virtually any question in seconds simply by typing it into a search engine, people don't need to think through as many problems on their own anymore. They're increasingly reliant on cut-and-paste, canned answers.

The problem is, because today's business world is so complex, your employees are going to run into brand-new problems on a regular basis. When they can extrapolate they'll be better prepared to turn these instances into opportunities to advance, create, and innovate.

What we're saying is, get your employees in the habit of proactively taking what they know and making it work for the company in new areas. Here are a few examples of how you might do that:

- Ask your employees to spend some time thinking about your competitors, and even businesses in totally different industries. What's working well for them? Can they think of ways to improve on it or take it a step further? Is there some aspect of what your competitors are doing that you can apply to your business? Have a regular meeting with employees that keeps this discussion flowing.

- When employees make a mistake, encourage them to consider whether the lesson they learned could also be applied to another part of the company.

- Ask employees to help you reassess how the company is structured and organized. Is there a way to synthesize two seemingly unrelated components in a way that adds value, solves a problem, or even creates a new revenue stream? For instance, could your marketing folks compile your sales or production team's best practices into written material (blog posts, or even a book!) that drives sales? Could underused production equipment be easily modified to create a new product?

Here's an example of how Barefoot used extrapolation to our advantage: Every time one of our wines won a gold medal at a competition, we hustled to print shelf signs for our sales staff, our distributors, and our retailers, and we placed gold medal stickers on the bottles. Sounds simple, we know, but nobody explicitly *told* us to "brag" on our winning wines. While placing gold medal stickers on wine bottles is common practice in the industry now, at that point, we were pioneers. All we knew was that we were pretty impressed by that shiny gold medal, and we figured our customers would be too—so we devised a way to validate their purchases by letting them know that they were picking a winner.

Another example of how extrapolation helped us grow centers around the fact that in the early days, our unproven wines were relegated to the bottom shelf where most new items are placed. Problem was, at ankle level, they were often overlooked by shoppers. We needed a way to drive foot traffic to where the Barefoot bottles were hiding. So that's exactly what we did. We took that expression and made it literal by creating foot-shaped decals called Sticky Feet. Our staffers would lay them on store floors down the wine aisle, leaving a trail that stopped right in front of Barefoot. And if a store would allow us, we'd start the trail all the way at the front door. You probably won't be surprised to hear that wherever Sticky Feet went down, sales went up.

The ability to extrapolate is so important in today's business world that it's something you should look for when you're hiring. Look for learners who can apply lessons in one area to a new one. Seek out individuals who don't need an example for everything, who are proactive about moving forward, who won't need your explicit guidance every step of the way, and who can anticipate a need and take the action necessary while preempting undesirable consequences.

When everyone in your organization can think of a way to *be* the example instead of waiting for the right one to come along, you'll be well on your way to success.

Chapter Fourteen

Know the difference between customer service and complaint resolution

These days, most companies have anything ranging from one person to a whole department dedicated to so-called "customer service." But let's be honest: For many of these departments truly gratifying service isn't on the menu. They're more like "complaint resolution" departments. They take calls or answer emails from unhappy customers and then try to resolve the problem as quickly as possible (often relying on a script or protocol), then move on to the next.

It's understandable. Dealing with unhappy customers isn't anyone's idea of fun. But the desire to "solve" their problems as quickly and painlessly (for you and your employees) as possible might actually be doing your company a disservice. Remember, happy customers are the lifeblood of your business and also one of your most valuable potential marketing tools, so no one at a company should rest until customers are impressed...not just satisfied. That means going *way* above and beyond merchandise exchanges and money-back guarantees.

Here's how we recommend handling customer service:

- **Give it away.** We recommend winning your disappointed customers back by giving your employees room to offer them free products and/or services. That's because when you only refund unhappy customers the money they paid, they'll proceed to take their business elsewhere in the future. After all, you've given them only what's due to them; not a compelling reason to stay. However, when you give customers free goods and services instead of, or even on *top* of, the refund, you're saying, "We care about what you think! Please give us another chance to show you that we can exceed your expectations!"

  And your employees will appreciate this approach, too. You're showing them you trust them to use their best thinking to handle customer complaints and to do what they think is necessary to satisfy the customer. When you show them you trust them to think on their feet and assess these kinds of situations, it will help them develop and hone their entrepreneurial thinking skills.

- **Start a conversation.** Get your employees in the habit of seeing customer service as a way for your company to get real and timely feedback about your goods and services from the people who are actually using them. Train employees to ask about the customer's experience with your company's products, where they bought them, how much they paid, how it performed for them, etc., and to really listen to the answers. This information is priceless for your production and marketing people because it will enable them to meaningfully improve your products and communication—which, in turn, could make the difference in your company staying relevant. So make sure your employees are proactive about starting these conversations and encourage them to share questions that get great feedback from customers with each other.

- **Look for ways to make customers happy.** Yes, of course your employees should strive to win customers back whenever they're dissatisfied. But no one at your company should just be sitting around and waiting for problems to arise. Encourage your employees to proactively think about what the company can do every day to make customers happy. These solutions don't have to be difficult or complex. For example, at Barefoot, we thought of store displays as "retail entertainment." We added color, fun, and seasonal theme sets for the enjoyment of our customers as they shopped. And if these displays naturally caught new shoppers' eyes...so much the better! Again, this is another great discussion to constantly be having with your employees. Encourage them to share their ideas for creating happier customers—no matter how crazy! You never know what's going to work.

- **Make customer service part of every employee's job description.** Ensure that everyone in your organization, from your receptionist to your office people, from your salespeople to your delivery people, and from your service people to your cashiers, knows where the money that pays their paycheck really comes from: Your customer! At Barefoot, new hires got an organization chart that showed the customer *on top*, as well as a "money map" that showed how the money came from the customer through the distribution channels, paid all the bills, and wound up in their paychecks.

  Anyone with any customer contact should be ready to give sincere personalized attention: acknowledging the customer's presence, making eye contact, addressing them by name, and conducting business in a helpful, friendly and personable manner. We suggest putting some teeth in this relationship by introducing incentives and bonuses based on sales, growth, and company profits.

- **Expand the definition of "customer."** When they hear the word "customer," your employees probably think about the end recipient of your company's product: the person who hands over the cash in order to take the merchandise home. At Barefoot, though, we found it helpful to broaden our definition of "customer," and thus, "customer service." Specifically, we considered everyone who bought or handled Barefoot to be a customer: In addition to shoppers, that included distributors, brokers, retailers, etc. We knew that each entity that touched Barefoot, from the winery to the shopper, "bought" it for a different reason. We tried to address each buyer's needs while providing them with speedy service, product availability, and friendliness, because if dealing with Barefoot was easy and profitable, that meant it would be more widely available for the shoppers who wanted to buy it. It also meant more sales and profits for us, too!

Ultimately, customers who call in with "complaints" represent less than 1 percent of the customers who are unhappy with your product, and who are now purchasing elsewhere. Try to head off as many complaints (voiced and unvoiced!) as possible by developing entrepreneurial-thinking employees who seek to over-deliver to all of your customers.

And here's something everyone at your company should remember: When someone *does* call in or comment with a complaint, you're fortunate to have the opportunity to hear what they think because their opinion can help your marketing, products, and services improve. (How else would you know what you're doing wrong?) Best of all, these re-wooed customers are the most likely to become advocates for your products and services because they have already demonstrated a propensity for talking about them. Why not keep these customers talking? Only this time, as advocates!

Chapter Fifteen

There's no substitute for face-to-face relationships

For anyone in the business world, technology ceased to be optional years ago. And most of the time, that's a good thing. Email, texting, social media, video chats, and more help us to connect instantaneously with a much (much!) wider range of people.

But there's a downside to the "technology takeover," too. Increasingly, genuine human connections are being replaced by mouse-clicks, keystrokes, and screen swipes. And the problem is, no matter how advanced technology becomes, it will *never* be a substitute for in-person interaction.

If you or any of your employees grew up with a cell phone in hand and a computer on the desk, it may be tempting to write this advice off as too old-fashioned. It's not. We certainly recognize the importance of digital resources, but we just want to caution you to use them appropriately as tools, and not let them become crutches— and that's precisely what you should be advising your employees.

To illustrate, even if we'd had social media, our blog, Skype, email, etc. at our disposal from the beginning, the Barefoot brand would never have become a national bestseller. That achievement required meetings, phone calls, and recurring personal visits that kept relationships all over the country healthy and up-to-date. The same thing will be true when your employees are working to build relationships inside and outside your company. No matter how tech-savvy they are, the truth is that high touch will beat high tech every time. Here are a few reasons why:

- **The time investment shows you really care.** In essence, an investment of time says, "While there are many other things I *could* be doing, I'm choosing to spend my time with you. That's how important I think you are!" Minutes and hours spent with another person have the power to create a bond that money can't buy. Plus, visiting someone repeatedly over a period of time can also provide valuable non-verbal clues to his or her values and concerns.

- **You're better able to give personalized attention.** Seriously, when someone is sitting behind a computerized command center, how much personalized attention can they really give a client? While they're talking on the phone, they might also be scrolling through their inbox. Or in the midst of writing a report for a client, the majority of their mind is already on the meeting that's supposed to happen in 15 minutes. Or they completely misread a customer's tone in an email, and only end up making her angry with their response. Or they simply tend to think of clients as account numbers instead of actual people because they never see their faces.

    Guess what? That stuff is much less likely to happen when you deal with clients face-to-face. It's hard to multi-task on something unrelated when someone is physically planted in front of you, demanding your attention. Unless you have no problem with blatant rudeness, you're focusing on the other person, responding not only to what they say, but also to their mood, movements, and many other non-verbal signals. You have the highest possible odds of determining what your client needs and how to deliver it—setting you up for the most success.

- **People want to do business with people they know.** More specifically, people want to do business with people they know *and* like. It's like how you keep going back to the same local restaurant again and again. You're comfortable there, you like the staff, the prices are reasonable, and the food is great. Why would you stop showing up (or recommending this restaurant to your friends!) just because a new establishment opened up down the street?

  Your employees' goal is to become the favorite restaurant in this story—but they can only do that if they develop a genuine, friendly relationship with clients while delivering consistent value. And trust us—that's extremely unlikely to happen if they keep their business relationships digital. Teach your employees that long-lasting loyalty requires a commitment to getting to know each client the old fashioned way.

- **You're more effective in general.** When you're talking to someone else in real time, you can make progress in real time and solve problems in real time. (Believe it or not, lobbing emails back and forth isn't always the most efficient method!) Thanks to facial expressions, body language, and tone of voice, you'll usually find out more than just the basics when you have a verbal conversation. In fact, employees who are especially observant may notice things about the other company or clients that they themselves aren't even aware of!

- **Make sure your employees understand that it's not a bad thing for their vulnerability to show.** In the virtual world, we can almost totally control the image we show to other people. We choose the pictures we post on our profile. We censor the information we do and don't want to share in our messages, posts, and updates. And usually, we can think about and edit what we want to say before pressing "send." But in a real-time, face-to-face relationship, the other person can see us in 3-D and observe our dynamic, spontaneous behavior, as well as our human imperfections. These make us appear more believable and sincere. And trust us, most people will overlook minor foibles in appearance and speech because you are *literally* there for them. It's special! This can be a big advantage in the long run. And in the short run, your employees will likely take precedence over virtual relationships.

- **Your online relationships will be enhanced.** When your employees have a strong personal connection with a client, their online relationship will automatically become more meaningful. Your company's fans will be more likely to retweet, post positive comments, and refer your business to their friends because they'll have a vested interest in seeing your company succeed.

Moral of the story? Always encourage your employees to meet clients and other key players in person when they can. When an important client or critical team member is on the other side of the globe, a face-to-face meeting once or twice a year can often be a smart investment. The rest of the time, if your communication is anything beyond a simple FYI, be sure to Skype or call.

Chapter Sixteen

Make organization a priority

I't's a fact that some people are naturally organized, and some aren't. It's also a fact that at least a basic (and preferably high) level of organization is necessary for your employees to put forth their best work. When they can organize their space, their time, their files, their thoughts, etc., it becomes much easier for them to over-deliver on the level of quality and service they're providing to your customers. And when they aren't in a constant state of anxiety over what they may or may not be forgetting, an important file they've lost, or a client meeting they've missed, they'll be able to devote more of their entrepreneurial thinking to making your company even better.

Here are some organizing "biggies" to help them get started:

- **Organize your space.** In Barefoot's early days, our "office" was the laundry room of the farmhouse we rented. But you know what? Humble as it may have been, that laundry room was Barefoot's designated place to do business. And we kept it tidy and organized as a result. Make sure your employees are doing the same with their workspaces. There is no excuse for being a slob at work. They can protest, "There's a method to my madness" all they want, but the truth is, no one does their best work in a cluttered, chaotic space. Having "a place for everything and everything in its place" will increase efficiency while cutting down confusion and the potential for conflict with their co-workers. And what if a potential client happens to catch a glimpse of an employee's messy office? A clean, ordered space will inspire a lot more confidence than an overflowing trash can and a desk littered with raggedy piles of paperwork.

- **Organize your time.** There are many workplace distractions. That's why it is so essential for your employees to carefully structure how they approach their workdays. One great way to do this is by using a prioritized to-do list. You might also encourage your employees to save their email checking for certain times each day. When they can organize their time, they'll be able to devote more of their attention to the task at hand.

- **Organize your files.** These days, most companies are paper/ digital hybrids. But no matter how information is distributed, your employees should have an accessible, intuitive system for organizing their files, be they memos, proposals, budgets, expense reports, etc. They should definitely not be stuffing all their paperwork into the same drawer or counting deleting a couple of emails as being organized. The more efficiently they can navigate their filing system, the less time that will be wasted, and the less chance they'll accidentally overlook or lose something important.

- **Organize meetings *before* they happen.** Especially if an employee is a casual and gregarious person, he or she may be tempted to "wing" client meetings. But remember, your company's credibility and success derive primarily from the way your employees present themselves and your products, so don't leave anything to chance. Whether they'll be meeting face-to-face, via video chat, or even talking on the phone, your employees should do their homework in advance.

If there are any gaps in their knowledge, make sure they've done the research to fill them. Standardize a process in which employees write out an agenda and have any necessary paperwork or materials at their fingertips. Make "be prepared" a company motto.

Encourage employees to think about the outcomes they want from the meeting before it starts, and to share those goals with the client. Have employees set start and end times, and make an announcement when they are halfway through. And throughout meetings, make sure one of your employees is listening for and writing down all action items. (We once had a mentor who said, "Don't take notes; make appointments and deadlines." That's solid gold advice!)

Yes, this may sound very regimented, but guess what? That's why it works. Your customers will appreciate the clarity and consistency they enjoy when interacting with your employees.

- **Organize your processes, procedures, and protocols.** In other words, record and disseminate everything about how your company works. Don't rely on memory, tradition, or word of mouth. You may *think* that "you'll always remember how to avoid this mistake in the future" or that "everyone knows that type of report's chain of custody" ...but what if you're wrong? It's always best to have a written record in order to avoid memory lapses, mistakes, confusion, and excuses.

For instance, in its first years of going national, Barefoot had a lot of chain store "disasters" ranging from distributors delivering the wrong shipments to barcodes being programmed incorrectly to shipments being forgotten in storerooms to displays being damaged—and much more. For almost three years, our expansion was stop-and-go as we learned to anticipate and navigate the nuances of each chain that carried our wines. What finally enabled us to get some control was simple: meticulous record-keeping and organization.

Essentially, we made lists of potential hazards and solutions, chain by chain, store by store. The lists got longer as our people got more experience, and as they experienced more problems. Their solutions included sending Barefooters to follow wine into a new store to make sure the orders got processed. Barefooters also helped clerks build displays where it was legal, and they took a bottle to the register to be sure the bar code scanned. Sounds simple enough, but if these staffers hadn't had written checklists and instructions, we would have had to solve the same problems over and over again. We would have wasted a lot of time, and more importantly, we probably would have lost a lot of business.

- **Organize your goals.** When most people think about organization, they think about the here and now: things that can be seen, touched, and immediately influenced. But your employees should also apply organization to their futures. It's not enough to simply have goals. If they don't break those goals down into a plan that's easily understood and executed, they may never achieve them. And worse yet, they won't have a clear picture of what they want to accomplish for your company. Here are some tips and strategies that have served us well over the years:

  ○ **Identify your incomplete goals.** What goals do you have that are yet to be achieved? Are they still relevant? It's important for employees to check in with their long- and short-term goals on a regular basis to make sure those goals are still steering them where they'd like to go.

○ **Write down your annual goals.** Employees should take a look at all of their long-term business goals. (When we say long-term, we don't suggest going beyond five years, because you can't reliably plan much farther ahead than that.) Then, they should break those goals down into annual goals.

○ **Set your deadlines.** Now, they should identify achievable milestones to be completed by certain dates. (We like using three-day holiday weekends for this purpose, since they naturally break up the year *and* give you something to look forward to.) For example, maybe an employee wants to get a promotion by Memorial Day, or meet a sales goal by Labor Day. They should post these deadlines on the calendar so that they stay on track. (In fact, it might be fun to have a calendar that features all of your employees' big goals.)

○ **Figure out the lead times.** Contrary to what you may have heard, the last minute is *not* the best minute. Nobody does their best work when they're stressed and scrambling to complete everything on time. So whether they're preparing for a big event or taking "baby steps" toward a bigger goal, your employees should calculate about how long it will take for them to prepare. They should look to see if there are overlaps with any other events or goals. By working backwards from these events, they will see when they must begin preparations.

○ **Plan your weeks.** Now that your employees have an accurate idea of what they need to do by which date, they should zoom-focus on each week. They should prioritize what needs to happen within the next seven days, and focus on items at the top of the list first. And they should roll any low-priority tasks that don't get accomplished to the next week.

We could write a whole book on the importance and how-tos of organization in business. But since this book is about far more than organization, we'll end this chapter here and leave you with this bottom line: No matter who you are or what you do, if you want to be successful in business, leave as little as possible up to chance. Have a place and a plan for everything.

Chapter Seventeen

Get serious about time management

Chances are, some of your employees may suffer from an 8 to 5 mentality. Instead of spending all their time working efficiently and effectively, they watch the clock. They get bogged down in responding to emails or performing other less-essential tasks. They distract your other employees.

And truthfully, from time to time, we all struggle to stay on task. It's often the case that fat gets built into our workdays—aimless meetings, endless emails, time by the water cooler—allowing us to make the march from 8 to 5 without being as effective as possible.

It's up to leaders to keep employees focused on getting things done. It's the best way to make the most of one of your most valuable resources—your employees!

The truth is, we all have a complicated relationship with our to-do lists. On the one hand, it's the roadmap that will enable us to reach our goals. And many of the items on it are things we're *really* looking forward to. However, on the other hand, it seems to grow without our permission, and we feel like we're constantly playing catch-up. And, of course, along with those tasks we're looking forward to, there are those things listed that we're absolutely dreading and (even though we may not want to admit it) that we're actively avoiding.

Make no mistake: Your employees are facing the same to-do list dilemma. When you help them improve their time management skills—by, among other things, teaching them the importance of schedules, a *prioritized* to-do list, and meeting deadlines—everyone is able to work more efficiently and effectively. The company runs more smoothly, and everyone wins.

With that in mind, here are some tactics to help everyone at your company start attacking your to-do lists in a timely manner:

- **Be honest about procrastination.** Sometimes we all put off tasks we know will be time-consuming, difficult, or both. What does that look like for you? Do you log into Facebook every time you begin to feel overwhelmed? Do you tend to spend a half-hour organizing your inbox so that you can feel productive, all the while ignoring a much more important (and much more intimidating) activity? Do you "accidentally" schedule off-site meetings whenever a certain unpleasant semi-monthly task comes up? You need to be honest with yourself about how and why you procrastinate so that you can begin to correct these behaviors. Along those lines, here's a solid-gold tip we got from a great mentor: Tackle the worst job first, and the rest of the list will be easy!

- **Remove distractions, especially during crunch time!** Even though it may not be pleasant to carry out, this tactic is important *and* effective. If you know that social media sites are your weakness, get an app or program that blocks how much time you can spend on them. If you're tempted to hop out of your chair and find someone to chat with, close your office door and hang a "do not disturb" sign on it. If you have 45 minutes to complete a report, close your email and web browser windows, and mute your phone. And be sure to turn off the "you've got mail" notice, which is notorious for sending us off on different tangents! Remember, it's not about multitasking here, it's about concentration!

- **Get comfortable with an "act now" way of thinking.** Think of yourself as a ball on a hill. If you aren't actively pushing that ball forward, it will begin to roll backward. That's because, in the real world, you can't push "pause" and stay where you are until you're comfortable with taking the next step. No, we're not saying that you should act without consideration or preparation. Learning and planning are both legitimate components of taking action. We're just making the point that in today's competitive business world, you don't have the luxury to avoid decisions that make you uncomfortable, or to postpone acting until the horizon is totally clear. Remember, an imperfect action taken now is better than no action taken at all, because it helps you maintain momentum, and it gets you in the habit of seizing fleeting opportunities.

  To ease into an "act now" way of thinking, start small. Challenge yourself to answer that passive-aggressive email you've been avoiding. Go to a colleague's office and deliver that uncomfortable, but necessary, feedback. Just do *something*. Then work up to the bigger things.

- **Prioritize, then prioritize some more.** Since you can't do everything at once, you need to make sure that you're always tackling the most important tasks first. Step one is simple: Make sure your to-do list exists in physical (or digital) form, not just in your mind. Then, assign each item a deadline and an "importance rating." For instance, tasks that are urgent might be assigned an "A." Tasks that are important, but not crucial, might get a "B." And tasks that can be pushed to the back burner or assigned to someone else altogether might get a "C." Admittedly, this example is simplistic—but you get the idea!

Now that you know what you have to do, when each task is due, and how important each one is, you can use your to-do list to ensure that you're using your time wisely. If you have an "A" on your list that needs to happen by the end of the day, don't allow yourself to get distracted by the "C"-rated email that just came through—or by any other shiny ball that might roll your way. Yes, it might take awhile to get used to working purposefully instead of reactively, but we promise you'll see major results in no time. We're also willing to bet that the gnawing feeling of anxiety that comes from having looming deadlines and incomplete projects will also soon dissipate!

- **Build in some breaks.** You and your employees are people, not machines. No matter how much is on your to-do list, you still need downtime (even fun time!) in order to allow your brains to rest and recharge. In fact, studies show that regular breaks actually enable you to be more creative and productive![1] So several times throughout the day (and especially if you're feeling particularly burned out and stressed), do something enjoyable. Take a stroll around the building. Enjoy an ice cream cone. Trade jokes with co-workers.

  Also, take a real live vacation every now and then! It's a good idea to plan your vacations at the beginning of the year and buy non-refundable tickets. (Yes, really!) They'll cost you less, and they'll force you to take the vacation. Plus, looking forward to your getaway will help you focus on completing your tasks before you go.

  At Barefoot, breaks were an essential part of our success strategy. From "Barefoot Days" (paid three-day weekends), to a paid day off on your birthday, to creating an office atmosphere that allowed people to have fun, we believed that all work and no play really did make Jack a dull boy.

You may have heard many of these tips before. If you've been resisting any of them up to this point, now's the time to stop. The more effectively and efficiently you use your time, the better off your company will be. Don't you want to do everything in your power to make sure that happens?

[1.] Phyllis Korkki, "To Stay on Schedule, Take a Break," *The New York Times,* 16 June 2012, accessed 14 August 2014, http://www.nytimes.com/2012/06/17/jobs/take-breaks-regularly-to-stay-on-schedule-workstation.html?_r=2&.

Chapter Eighteen

Always over-deliver

Today's consumers are more informed than ever. With the click of a mouse, they can compare prices, read reviews, and find customer service horror stories. And they're using that information. They don't just go with the least expensive option. They look for value—how can they get the best experience for the best price. And that's why it's so important that everyone at your company over-deliver to your customers, every time.

At Barefoot, we always strove to over-deliver by meeting and exceeding customers' expectations in quality, quantity, and customer service. Prioritizing our customers' experience over our own comfort and (sometimes) potential solvency wasn't always easy, but it did pay off. Our customers were satisfied and remained loyal, and our company grew. Here are some principles we followed that you should instill in the way your employees (and you!) work with your customers:

- **Never compromise on quality.** A product's packaging, pricing, and reputation all send the consumer signals about its value. If it lives up to those "brand promises" of quality, the customer is validated in his decision to buy. And until the price goes up, the quality goes down, or the packaging becomes more corporate or generic, he'll remain loyal. The point? Consistent quality and value is king. Make sure your employees are checking and double checking quality every chance they get.

On more than a few occasions at Barefoot, the opportunity to save money on production and materials presented itself—but we nearly always turned these opportunities down because they would have affected the final product.

For example, an accountant once figured out that we could save $0.09 per wine bottle by using gold ink instead of gold foil on the label, and by reducing the quality of our corks. At the time, we were selling 300,000 cases per year with 12 bottles in each case, resulting in 3,600,000 bottles. At $0.09 per bottle, the accountant concluded, our total savings would be $324,000.

The problem behind the accountant's suggestion was the basic assumption that sales would remain at 300,000 cases per year (or more). They wouldn't, because sales were, and still are, based on a perception of quality and authenticity. Gold foil and high quality corks validated the consumer's purchase and gave us a market advantage at our low everyday price point. Needless to say, we continued to use gold foil and high-quality corks.

- **Focus on providing excellent customer service.** How we are treated when things go wrong is more important than how we are treated when things go right. It's when we see a company's true colors and decide whether or not to continue buying their products. Reputation is based on excellent customer service—so make sure your employees are always going above and beyond.

- **Always tell the truth.** At Barefoot, we made the decision to always tell the truth no matter how painful it might be. That's because a crucial part of over-delivering is doing what's best for your customer (and being honest is always what's best!).

We remember one situation in which Barefoot had put the wrong barcode on a store's shipment of cabernet, which meant that the wine rung up for less than it should have. In this instance, it was our team who caught the mistake, not the customer. We could have kept our mouths shut, hoping that our error would remain unnoticed. But as soon as possible, Michael showed up at the store's corporate office with a check for the store's loss, plus the time and expense of dealing with the mistake. Then he described to the manager in detail how we at Barefoot were changing our internal processes to make sure that the bar code problem would never happen again. And guess what? That store thanked us for doing the right thing, and it didn't stop ordering from us.

- **Always share third party endorsements.** As consumers, we all want to know that when we give our loyalty to a brand, we're making a smart decision. So anytime you receive awards, accolades, and endorsements, have your employees share the news in as many places as possible: on the website, on the marketing materials, in their conversations with people outside the company, and even on your product's packaging, to name just a few possibilities. And do it as quickly as possible! Consumers want *current* validation. This is an easy (and gratifying!) way to deliver that validation to your customers.

Remember, your brand's reputation is a very valuable—and very fragile—thing. If any of your employees under-deliver, your brand will be damaged, possibly beyond repair. But when your products and services meet or exceed customers' expectations, they are more likely to remain loyal and recommend your brand to friends, family, and associates.

Chapter Nineteen

Always ask yourself, "How would I like it?"

In the hustle and bustle of today's business world, there's no such thing as a slow day. And when we're really busy and stressed to the max it can be easy to forget how we treat people. But the reality is, relationships have never been more important. From vendors to clients to employees, building strong relationships is back in vogue, and it has to be a priority for everyone at your company.

A great way to ensure everyone at your company is committed to building strong relationships is to constantly ask, "How would I like it?"; otherwise known as the Golden Rule for business professionals.

The idea is that when you put yourself in the other person's shoes and look at your company from a different perspective, you'll get an objective view of your business practices and how they might need to change in order for you to build a brand you'd be loyal to and that employees would feel proud to uphold.

It baffles us that many businesses don't appear to follow this formula, because it's so simple and so reliable. Instead, they limit their success by allowing fear, greed, prejudices, or the way other companies do things to guide their decisions. Don't join them. Consistently ask yourself these questions:

Question One: Would I work for myself? Specifically:

- Would I want to work for an employer who treated my labor as a commodity, trying to see how little I would work for? Or would I prefer an employer who sees people as assets, rewarding them for performance and acknowledging their achievements?

- As an employer, do I acknowledge producers publicly, or am I afraid they will ask for a raise? Do I think that giving time off will cause me to increase or lose production? Do I see medical and retirement benefits as a cost, or as an investment in long-term stability?

Yes, it can be scary to let go of even a single extra dollar when your budget isn't what you'd like it to be. But tightfistedness could tip the balance toward your company's failure due to the costs of turnover as well as untapped innovation and talent. When Barefoot began paying for performance rather than attendance, we found our best people didn't leave because they benefited financially from their own production. Those who were less productive were paid less and could not afford to stay.

Question Two: Would I trust myself? Specifically:

- Would I trust someone who holds back relevant information, who ignores me, and who is difficult to reach? Or would I prefer someone who sees me as a strategic business partner, keeps me up to date, shares challenges and opportunities, and understands my goals?

- As a leader, am I open and honest with employees about where the company stands, what challenges we're facing, and what I want? Do I volunteer updates regarding our growth and plans? Do I keep employees up to date on the good and the bad? And on a basic level, am I friendly or hostile?

Question Three: How would I like selling to myself? Specifically:

- If I were a vendor and had two clients, one who treated me with respect and dignity, and another who viewed me as a necessary evil (and maybe even thought I was a huckster or trickster), which one would get preferential treatment? With which would I share what I know about their competition?

- As an employee of this company, do I take time to see sales-people, listen to what they have to offer, and treat them like strategic partners? Or do I put them off with an "it's just an-other salesperson trying to sell me something, and they can wait" attitude?

- Do I give suppliers, vendors and others outside the company advance warning when the company won't be able to make a payment on time?

It's absolutely essential that you and your employees treat ven-dors in a way that honors the relationship. Suppliers, vendors, bank-ers, and other third parties you and your employees must work with to keep your company running usually aren't unaccommodating bad guys. They want you to succeed because when you grow, they grow. Once we realized that these third parties were people with fears and goals just like ours, it was much easier for us to be transparent, in-formative, and proactive...which helped Barefoot to maintain good relationships with them.

Part of your company's standard should be that suppliers, vendors, and others outside your company are treated with the utmost respect. In fact, at Barefoot, we always treated our vendors and their salespeople as if they were part of our staff. We saw them as valuable allies who could significantly influence our bottom line—and often, they did! Turns out when you're a favorite client, you get nice perks.

For instance, the salesperson calling on you may have special "pocket" deals to help close new customers or gain larger orders, such as reduced interest rates or extended terms. Give salespeople a reason to offer these to you instead of to your competition! And even if they can't offer you a deal outright, they can still be your advocate for better terms with their companies. And don't forget about the value of information, either. Salespeople can help you to anticipate a competitor's move, or to be prepared for a new opportunity or a change in laws or business practices. After all, it's part of their job to stay on top of the ever-changing marketplace!

Question Four: Would I buy from myself? Specifically:

- Would I buy from a company that treated me like a pain in the neck if I had a problem with their product, or would I prefer to buy from a company that thanked me for bringing my concerns to their attention? Would I buy a product that previously tricked me with false claims, fancy packaging, and an amazing (but too-good-to-be-true) price? Or would I be loyal to a product that demonstrated time-tested value?

- Does my business continually strive to offer a product or service that holds its value over time? Do we do everything in our power to make sure that customers don't choose to shop for an alternative? Does my company tend to see customers only as walking dollar signs, or do we give each client personal attention before and after their purchases?

At Barefoot, we believed that customers look for overall value when buying a product, not just a low price. That's why we turned down opportunities to cut costs and labor many times. We felt that these measures (which touched on everything from packaging to pricing to the wine itself) would reduce the customer's perception of Barefoot's quality.

At the same time, we continually looked for ways to let customers know that we cared about them and that putting their faith in us was a good decision. We over-delivered on customer service. We validated the consumer's decision to choose our brand by publicizing all of our awards, accolades, and endorsements. And we took every opportunity to get feedback on what people liked about Barefoot, and how they thought we could make it better.

No matter what industry or field you're in, the most critical decisions you'll make as a leader will be shaped by your attitude toward your employees and by how that attitude affects how they treat people outside the company. So make sure the question, "How would I like it...?" is never far from your mind.

Chapter Twenty

The customer buys *you* more than your product

If your employees aren't keeping this mantra top of mind, you could be in trouble.

It doesn't matter how unique, useful, or all-around amazing a product is if the person selling it is disagreeable. Think about it: Chances are, you've stopped patronizing a store or restaurant because of rude or unprofessional staff. Why should your company's customers, or your distributors' customers, be any different?

That's why it's crucial for you to honestly assess your employees' customer service skills and determine the type of impression they're making on potential clients. Throughout Barefoot's history, we were hardly the only wine label with whom retailers could do business. Before we could get our wines on the shelves and in front of our target buyer, we had to get our salespeople, distributors, and distributors' salespeople excited about our product. And in retrospect, we are convinced that if we hadn't focused on "hand selling" Barefoot to each customer, so to speak, our brand would never have made it. (Hand selling, by the way, is actually being there face to face with the customer, explaining your product's benefits, and offering it to them by hand.)

The truth is, conventional distribution systems are overloaded with products, and many of them—no matter how deserving—get lost in the shuffle. So don't rely solely on your product to succeed. Your employees must also work on distinguishing themselves in the eyes of customers. Here's how to do that:

- **Pay attention to your facial expressions...** Facial expressions are an invaluable way through which to express sincerity, interest, curiosity, happiness, and more—so coach your employees to leave the poker face at home. Also, closely observing the other person's expressions can give instant feedback about how the message is being received. Your employees can quickly adjust their message on the spot to make it more meaningful or agreeable, and to avoid possible misunderstandings.

- **...And your body language...** As humans and social animals, we are naturally wired to convey our feelings and attitudes through the way we stand, sit, gesture, and more. Still, it's a good idea for your employees to spend a little time learning the basics of body language. For instance, if they know that hands in one's pockets indicate boredom or disinterest, whereas leaning slightly forward indicates interest, they'll be able to respond more accurately to others *and* avoid sending messages they don't mean to.

- **...And your tonality.** When spoken, the same words can have a very different meaning based on the tone, inflection, and emphasis that the speaker gives. Your employees should never forget that their tone of voice, inflection, and attitude can be "read" by customers, and they should speak accordingly. That goes for phone conversations as well as face-to-face meetings. So your employees should do whatever they need to do to have a happy, confident attitude before they pick up the phone. Throughout the conversation, they should make sure they are sitting up straight or standing. And always remind them that believe it or not, the person on the other end of the line can "hear" them smiling!

- **Give personalized attention.** Nobody wants to be just another face in the crowd, or worse yet, a number on an end-of-year report or profit sheet. Instead, customers want to feel that they are special, that they are valued as individuals, and that their needs, wants, and preferences have been taken into account. Coach your employees to ask customers about what products they like and why, and find out which ones they *don't* like and why. Everyone at your company should show an interest in customer concerns, and should always try to remember something about each person that they can bring up the next time they meet. During Michael's early days as a salesman, he was amazed by how surprised and pleased his clients were when he remembered that one of them was celebrating a special anniversary, or had recently adopted a dog, or was expecting a baby, for example.

- **Validate their decisions.** When they're buying a new product, customers want to be able to look your company's representative in the eye and hear what they think about it. They'll ask, *Have you tried it? Do you like it? Would you buy it again? How has it made your life better?* Most of all, customers want to be able to hear and feel *honesty* from your employees when they answer these questions.

The process of validation helps people make the decision to buy your product, or to buy more of your product. If you want your employees to be able to go the extra mile in validating a customer's decision to buy your product, we recommend that they be able to demonstrate a knowledge of similar products, and without bashing other brands, show how yours is superior or more appropriate for the customer's needs. Later, have employees follow up and ask your customers what their experience with the product has been like.

Bottom line: We're convinced that we were successful only because we placed a priority on developing healthy, friendly relationships with our customers, and on maintaining those relationships through regular conversations and follow-up. Yes, our customers loved Barefoot wines…but they also loved us.

Chapter Twenty-One

Don't take "no" for an answer

"**I**'m sorry, but my answer is no."

When you're running a company and hear the statement above, it's a motivator. You know you'll have to come back to the person and ask for their business again because your company's survival depends on it. Taking "no" for an answer simply isn't a luxury you have.

But for your employees, "no" can feel like a door slamming shut. So when they hear it from a prospective client, vendor, or maybe even you, they check that item off their list. After all, they tried. They assume that a rejection signals that they're at the end of the line.

One way to fight the I-gave-it-the-old-college-try mentality is to reward results instead of effort. Keep your employees focused on seeking solutions that lead to results rather than on simply moving from item to item on their to-do lists.

This lesson was really driven home for us not in a business setting, but at a Mexican restaurant with Bonnie's mother, Mabel. On this particular evening, Mabel was frustrated because she couldn't get the server to let her order veggie fajitas.

"I'm sorry, we only serve beef, chicken, or shrimp fajitas," she was told.

So Mabel asked sweetly (Solution #1!). No dice. She offered to pay extra (Solution #2!). Nope. Finally, she said, "All right. I'll have a chicken fajita, hold the chicken." (Solution #3!)

"No problem," the server said. (Success!)

Mabel taught us something important that night: You have to figure there's always an answer. Be persistent, and keep playing the game until you find it.

Make sure your employees understand that hearing "no" doesn't mean it's over. They shouldn't consider a task completed until they've gotten a positive result or at least exhausted every possible solution.

As we got Barefoot up and running, we were told "no" 20 times a day. But we never let it stop us. If we had, we never would have been able to get our business off the ground. We certainly wouldn't have been able to shake up the wine industry the way we did.

So, as we began to hire people, we made sure they wouldn't take "no" for an answer, either. Specifically, we instituted the "No Game" with our employees. We gave them the same advice we're giving you (and advice you should certainly pass on to your employees): From this moment on, erase "yes" and "no" from your business vocabulary, and replace those terms with "now" and "later." Consider this: Prospects can say "yes," but never give you the purchase order. Conversely, they can say "no," only to place an order months later. Do you see why "now" and "later" are the only two answers that matter?

So, here's the point: Instead of assuming that "no" signals a closed door, teach your employees to ask a different day, a different person, or a different way! Ask as many times as needed. And while you're at it, keep count. See how many "laters" are racked up before arriving at "now." In a nutshell, that's the No Game.

Believe it or not, the No Game became a huge motivator and morale booster for our salespeople at Barefoot. They cheerfully attacked rejections as though they were puzzles to solve. Soon, our people began to come back from sales calls bragging about who got the longest string of "nos" before hearing "yes." It wasn't even worth reporting until you got at least four. (If you're curious, the average number of "nos" we got was seven.)

We encourage you and your employees to play the No Game, too. You'll find that making a game out of rejection takes the frustration out of this particular challenge, and that it also encourages you to be more persistent and to seek solutions and results. If you know that the average number of "nos" is seven, for instance, you'll keep going at four, and at ten you'll feel like a positive answer is right around the corner. And guess what? Not only does the No Game keep your momentum going, it also hones everyone's sales skills (no matter what their position) because it forces them to continually change their tactics, approach new people, and develop the patience to wait for the "now."

Remember, in the majority of situations, *you* are the only person who can say no—because you are the only person who can stop asking. And your company's ultimate success might happen because of a well-earned "yes"! Ours did!

Chapter Twenty-Two

Say "thank you" to everyone—especially to your employees

In the hustle and bustle of leading a business, you probably don't always remember to say thank you. But making gratitude part of your culture plays an essential role in creating employees who feel empowered and engaged.

In truth, you should be saying thank you to everyone you come into contact with through your company. Everyone, from employees to colleagues to vendors, will respond positively when you say—or better yet, demonstrate—your thanks. For instance:

- "Thank you for choosing to do business with us. We know you have other options, so to express our gratitude for your loyalty, we'd like to offer you a 30 percent discount on your next order."

- "I really appreciate you taking the time to help our company improve our advertising campaign. I'd like to take you out to lunch one day to say thanks."

- "Thanks for agreeing to help us get the word out about our company. In return, we'd like to donate some products and help out at your events."

Obviously, these are just a few examples of how you might say thank you to the people you work with. And actually, a good portion of the advice we've given you in this book is about demonstrating gratitude through your actions and choices.

However, there's one type of thanks that can really make or break your business: the gratitude you express to (or withhold from) your employees. That's what we'd like to focus on here.

In a recent Gallup survey, 57 percent of disengaged employees said they felt ignored at work.[1] *Well, that doesn't sound like such a bad thing. After all, isn't that what employees want—to not be micromanaged, and to be left alone to do their jobs in peace without commentary from management?* you might ask. Not exactly. While nobody wants to hear a constant stream of criticism or anxiously delivered "suggestions" from the boss, workers *do* want to know that they're doing well, and that their efforts are valued. According to one *New York Times* commentator, "Regular praise...would go a long way toward getting the checked-out to check back in."[2] And we agree.

When your employees work hard on your company's behalf, they deserve your thanks and appreciation. Don't take it for granted when your employees put in extra hours, land a coveted client, or turn out an incredibly well-thought-out proposal, for example. For that matter, don't take for granted the fact that they show up to work at all, or make the mistake of believing that "just" a paycheck will make them happy. Many people reflexively see their jobs as an extension of family, with the bosses in the role of parental figures. Which means workers want to please their bosses, and they'd like to know when their bosses are pleased. Just like in a family.

The point is, make sure your people know that you have noticed their efforts and that you're grateful for their knowledge and help. In return you'll gain their buy-in, loyalty, enthusiasm, and over-and-beyond efforts. Acknowledgment and validation of stellar performance breeds more of it!

The best news is, saying thanks to your team really doesn't have to cost you much money, or even take up a lot of your time. It only takes a few seconds to say, "Samantha, I've noticed that you never leave work until you've returned all of your voicemails. Thank you for taking such good care of our clients." But in those few seconds, you've made Samantha's day and motivated her to keep providing excellent service to her clients.

At Barefoot, we constantly tried to catch our people doing something right, and when we did, we'd brag about it—to the whole staff. We'd send out written acknowledgments, and we also spotlighted each employee's achievements on his or her anniversary.

Specifically, we'd send out a memo describing how that employee organized the department, or boosted income, or just made other people's jobs easier. We'd make these announcements at staff meetings, too. We'd say, for instance, "Here's what Debbie did to save money for Barefoot and increase your bonus. This is why she's a good teammate." Then we would leave, and other employees would say, "Wow, we didn't know you did all that!"

Saying thanks in this way had three distinct benefits: First, it gave everyone the chance to talk together about their jobs, increasing their understanding of how and why Barefoot "worked." Second, it helped create a mutual respect amongst teammates. That's important, because people want to know that their colleagues, not just their bosses, appreciate the work they do every day. Having supportive colleagues can be a huge driving force in growing your employees' engagement, loyalty, and performance. And third, seeing each employee acknowledged on their anniversary inspired everyone else to do their own absolute best work so that they would receive lots of public praise when it was their turn in the spotlight!

Finally, a more labor-intensive (but well worth your while!) way to thank your people for all they do is to create a positive, supportive (and yes, fun!) company culture. We'll get to that in the next chapter. But first, take a break from reading and say thanks to an employee!

---

[1] Timothy Egan, "Checking Out," *The New York Times*, 20 June 2013, accessed 15 August 2014, http://opinionator.blogs.nytimes.com/2013/06/20/checking-out/?_php=true&_type=blogs&_r=0.

[2] Ibid.

Chapter Twenty-Three

Make it fun to work for you

It's indisputable that culture has a direct bearing on the survival and growth of a company. And it's also indisputable that culture starts from the top and permeates throughout an organization. That means it's up to you to determine what it's like to be an employee at your company. Here are our suggestions: Make it fulfilling, and make it *fun*.

There's a myth that when company cultures are serious and businesslike productivity improves. But the reality is, productivity improves when people enjoy being at work and enjoy the work they're doing.

Barefoot's culture was based on two overarching principles: *generosity* and *permission*. Our use of Worthy Cause Marketing, wherein we donated Barefoot's products and manpower to nonprofit organizations whose missions we believed in, gave employees a level of satisfaction that went far beyond making a sale—they got to make a difference. And by allowing, no, *insisting* that people use their imaginations to experiment, be creative, and even make mistakes, we gave them permission to be all they could be.

Now, let's talk about fun. Just as our goal was to create a wine brand that was more lighthearted than its "fancy, stuffy, and pretentious" peers, it was important to us that our people not feel that their jobs were all work and no play. We wanted our company to be a fun place to work—not unprofessional, but lighted-hearted, cheerful, and sometimes, a little silly.

That way, we figured, our people would stay fresh and involved. They'd look forward to coming to work, and because of that, they'd do their *best* work. Plus, injecting a regular dose of enjoyment into our employee's lives was a great way to thank them for helping us run, sustain, and grow our company.

Here are several specific ways in which Barefoot made being an employee fun.

- **We let employees choose their titles.** Foot-related names were encouraged for obvious reasons. Michael's business card said, "Head Stomper." Bonnie was "Original Foot." (Fun fact: the famous Barefoot label is based on her footprint!) Randy Arnold, our National Sales Manager, was "The Barefoot Guy." And Doug McCorkle, the company's Chief Financial Officer, was "The Cork," partly because of his name but also because, as the money guy, when a bad idea picked up speed he was the one who was expected to put a cork in it. People had conventional titles, too. The point was, put anything on your business card, just make sales happen.

- **We gave plenty of time off.** For obvious reasons, employees have positive feelings about an employer who says, "Hey, you know what? Why don't you take a day off? You deserve it. And it won't come out of your vacation or sick days." Not so obvious, but equally true, is that these unworked hours *won't* mean a loss of productivity and revenue.

  At Barefoot, we decided to give employees a Friday off during the three months each year that didn't already have a built-in three-day weekend. We found that these "Barefoot Days," as we called them, didn't hurt productivity at all. On the contrary, our folks regularly put in extra hours to finish their work *before* the three-day weekend. They didn't want to take their unfinished projects with them, worry about them while they were on holiday, or have to come back to them the following Monday. Best of all, when they returned, they were recharged, refreshed, and ready to get back to work.

But that's not all—Barefoot Days benefited the company for two additional reasons. First, you know how you tend to feel tense and fatigued after working for months on end without a break? Well, that long-haul stress became a thing of the past, because with Barefoot Days, work periods never lasted more than six weeks without a break. Attitudes and morale improved accordingly. Secondly, and perhaps most importantly, Barefoot Days created *major* employee engagement. Our people loved working for a company that told them to take more vacation, and as a result, they tended to be incredibly loyal and hardworking.

- **We celebrated birthdays.** After you hit a certain age (it's different for everyone, but we all get there!) birthdays stop being something you really look forward to. Partially, that's because we don't want to add another number to our ages. But also, it's because birthdays stop being special occasions. Sure, you might get a cake in the break room and a special dinner with your family, but by and large, your birthday is just another day in the ongoing grind.

Not so for Barefoot employees! At our company, everyone got their birthday off with pay, or a day they could float. That in itself isn't *especially* unusual, but Barefoot also gave the birthday folks $100 to spend. They were supposed to use it for themselves on something fun like a meal or a gift, not for paying the electric bill. That $100 did come with one requirement: People had to tell everyone what they spent their money on. No receipts necessary, just bring back a story. Soon, birthdays were back in style.

- **We didn't take ourselves too seriously.** As you're well aware by now, the Barefoot brand was not one that took itself seriously. We believed that you could—and should—have a great time with a bottle of wine even if you weren't an oenophile. So we tried to inject fun into how we "did" the wine business. Our store displays and marketing materials were colorful, festive, and designed to entertain consumers. And at tastings, we encouraged our people to create as much of a party feel as they could. Let's just say they succeeded—and that there were a lot of foot puns: "This will knock your socks off," "You'll be head over heels for Barefoot," "Try some wine with sole," etc.

Overall, not being bound to "businesslike" seriousness was therapeutic to our employees, especially if they came to us from a more "traditional" workplace. They loved that they could let their creative juices flow, and that they were encouraged to make our customers smile and laugh!

Essentially, here's what we hope you take away from this chapter, and what we hope you'll pass on to your employees: Just because it's work doesn't mean it can't also be fun.

The Entrepreneurial Culture

Workshops and Corporate Training to Engage and Empower Your People

P roven entrepreneurial thinkers, Michael and Bonnie started Barefoot, America's #1 wine brand, in a laundry room and grew it into a national bestseller. Learn how they achieved huge success by developing an entrepreneurial culture to engage and empower their people.

Here are just some of the ways Michael and Bonnie can help you create an entrepreneurial culture inside your organization, based on the **Guiding Principles for Success (GPS)**™:

- Ignite your next company-wide event with a keynote on entrepreneurial culture

- Empower your field managers with the tools they need to roll out an entrepreneurial culture

- Ensure implementation of entrepreneurial policies and procedures with key leaders

- Reinforce entrepreneurial culture with on-line sessions and Q&A opportunities

Book an entrepreneurial culture keynote, workshop, or corporate training session today at:

TheBarefootSpirit.com/BookUs.

Praise for Bonnie and Michael

"They have an ability to speak to any group of people in a way that resonates with their particular needs and through their stories the hard lessons of business are understood in an entertaining fashion. Because of the success of their talks [at The International Council for Small Business (ICSB) World Entrepreneurship Conference in Dublin], they have already been invited back to Ireland for other speaking engagements and I understand from international colleagues that invitations to other countries are also likely to happen."

~ Professor Thomas M. Cooney,
Chair of the ICSB 2014 Organising Committee,
College of Business, Dublin Institute of Technology

"I thoroughly enjoyed their presentation at the CEO Conference–wonderful job! They are great role models."

~ Dr. Gerald E. Hills,
Founder, Collegiate Entrepreneurs' Organization (C.E.O.)

"Michael and Bonnie's story tells the audience the all-too-brutal truth about what one really has to do to succeed."

~ Adam Hartung, Contributing Author, *Forbes*

"Bonnie and Michael were excellent keynote speakers for our inaugural entrepreneurs' awards luncheon. They tailored their presentation to fit the Chamber's mission and the audience's expectations. The duo's success story captured the audience's attention from the first sentence to the last word. Their presentation was informative, useful, and charismatic."

~ Darrell W. Randle,
Vice President, Small Business Development,
Mobile Area Chamber of Commerce

"Our entire group benefited from their wisdom. The fact they were so entertaining was simply icing on the cake. We are having them back!"

~ Patrick Snyder,
Executive Director, United States Association
for Small Business and Entrepreneurship (USASBE)

"The Barefoot Founders were a big hit at the recent Northwest SOCAP Chapter meeting in San Francisco. Michael Houlihan and Bonnie Harvey are truly charming and engaging presenters! They shared stories of the challenges they faced founding the Barefoot Wine brand and how they overcame them by putting the customer first and creatively responding to their needs and wants. Their tag team approach was refreshing and kept us entertained while delivering this important message. It was fun and our members had nothing but praise!"

~ Northwest Society of Consumer Affairs
Professionals in Business (SOCAP) Board

"We enjoyed listening to the lessons that they learned. The worthy cause marketing concept was worth the evening by itself."

~ David Torrance, President,
Renaissance Executive Forums Dallas;
Member, Dallas Area Chamber of Commerce

"Michael and Bonnie were great! It's hard to be the last speakers at a conference and they pulled it off. So many people commented on their presentation. They really are connected on a very special level. Well done!"

~ Pat Murphy, CEO,
The Institute for Social, Search & Mobile Marketing

"An excellent and inspiring presentation!"

~ Gavin Duffy, Entrepreneur;
Panelist, *Dragons' Den* Television Show

"It is so refreshing to hear the mindset behind such a great product and the evolution of your business. I will be able to take your business lessons and relay them back to those that are working to expand. I especially enjoyed your explanation of the 'money map' and 'organizational charts' but more importantly the idea of treating suppliers (and all others) how you would like to be treated. Such a basic idea that seems to fall by the wayside."

~ Gina L. Sederstrom, Financial & Portfolio Advisor,
Morris Fuller Group, Merrill Lynch Private Client Group

"Michael's reputation as a successful entrepreneur precedes him. He is on top of his topics and consistently delivers news we can use. He has given my staff sales tools and insights that have resulted in increased sales and a new appreciation for customer relations. He is clear, understandable and practical. He shares his real world business experience with passion and intensity. Nobody dozes off when Michael is speaking!"

~ Jeff Stevenson, Founder & CEO,
VinoPRO Inc. (2013 Inc. 500 Company)

About *The Barefoot Spirit*

The story of the little winery that broke all the rules and left its footprints across an industry.

When Michael Houlihan and Bonnie Harvey started Barefoot Wines in their laundry room in 1985, they had no money or experience, but they made up for that with creativity, resourcefulness, guts, and grit. By the time they sold the brand in 2005, they'd won a ton of awards and helped transform an entire industry from stuffy and intimidating to fun, casual, and socially aware. *The Barefoot Spirit* is a surprising, enlightening, and entertaining guidebook for anyone in business and a great read for anyone who loves a rags-to-riches tale. It's a case study, an idea book, and a snapshot of the American spirit, West Coast-style.

Ride along with Bonnie and Michael on a seat-of-your-pants business adventure and get a rare view behind the scenes of the wine industry.

Obtain your copy of the companion book, the *New York Times* business bestseller *The Barefoot Spirit: How Hardship, Hustle, and Heart Built America's #1 Wine Brand*, at TheBarefootSpirit.com.

Praise for *The Barefoot Spirit*

"A runaway bestseller. Whether they are Barefoot or have shoes on, it is a great, great book!"

~ Jeff Hayzlett, CEO, The Hayzlett Group;
CMO & VP, Eastman Kodak;
Contributing Editor, Bloomberg Television

"This is a warm, wonderful, inspiring book that entertains and motivates at the same time."

~ Brian Tracy, Motivational Speaker;
Entrepreneur and Success Expert; International Best Selling
Author of over 50 Books, including *Eat That Frog!*

"Great read, great book. This story is beyond wine and the love of wine; it's about starting a business."

~ Fran Tarkenton, NFL Quarterback and NFL and
Collegiate Football Halls of Fame Inductee; Entrepreneur;
Host, *The Fran Tarkenton Show* on Sirius XM Radio

"Started reading and really like the personalized style."
~ **Robert Reiss, Host,** *The CEO Show with Robert Reiss*
(nationally syndicated on AM/FM to 600,000 listeners);
Columnist, *Forbes*; **Chairman, The Conference Board's**
Senior Marketing Executive Conference

"This book is arguably the best book I have ever read that details the real life challenges that every business has in getting established and growing to a substantial size. More importantly, you should read the book, and after you've done that give it to some of your clients."
~ **Ric Payne, CEO, Principal**

"What I like best about the book is that Houlihan and Harvey lead by example, and explain how they took an idea and a little blood, sweat, and wine, and turned it into a multi-million dollar brand that is now a household name. Talk about a financial gold mine."
~ **Bryan Beatty, Certified Financial Planner and Partner,**
Egan, Berger & Weiner, LLC

"*The Barefoot Spirit* is full of great practical lessons for entrepreneurs."
~ **Kolie Crutcher, Founder & CEO,** *GET MONEY Magazine*

"It's an inspiration to see how they broke all the rules and still succeeded against all odds. For anyone contemplating starting a business, there are lessons to be learned here and an entertaining story as a bonus."
~ **Alan Caruba, Book Reviewer, National Book Critics Circle;**
Author and Columnist

"I try to read all the books of the authors on my show and am just getting into *The Barefoot Spirit*. It's one of the best books on entrepreneurship I've read."

~ Kip Marlow, Entrepreneur; Host, *Entrepreneurs Club Radio*

"Fun beach reading for small business inspiration. *The Barefoot Spirit* is an entertaining rags-to-riches story of American entrepreneurship. It's the first-hand tale of California rule breakers Michael Houlihan and Bonnie Harvey, founders of the country's top-selling wine brand."

~ Adrienne Burke, Writer, Yahoo! Small Business

"*The Barefoot Spirit* is the perfect wine beach read…"

~ Laura Lawson, Host, *The Wine Crush* Radio Show

"I picked up Michael and Bonnie's book chronicling the Barefoot story with the intention of a quick scan and found myself spending the better part of a Sunday thoroughly enjoying myself reading cover-to-cover. I believe students will find *The Barefoot Spirit* both a great read and an important lesson in creative problem solving in the face of critical challenges."

~ Pat Dickson, 2013 President, United States Association for Small Business and Entrepreneurship; Associate Professor, Wake Forest University, North Carolina

"It's an amazing story. Get a taste and a copy today!"

~ Susan Hyatt, Founder, Core Thought, Inc.; Author, *Strategy for Good*

"I pretty much gobbled it right down in one sitting. Having lived through many similar challenging circumstances in the wine biz, it was an inspiration. And I can see why the business community is embracing it as a customer service how-to."

~ Mark Chandler, Owner, Chandler & Company
Wine Consultancy

"*The Barefoot Spirit* will appeal to entrepreneurs, business people, non-profit leaders, and anyone who is passionate about activism, unlikely stories, and—oh yes—wine. In content, message, and even writing style, it's smart, funny, self-deprecating."

~ Michael Tate, Board President,
San Francisco Gay Men's Chorus

"When you have a passion but no formula to follow, *The Barefoot Spirit* will inspire and direct you and your energy. A book that shows those with the true entrepreneur's spirit how not to get stuck on the small things and make decisions from the soul. This book is as unpretentious as the wine they produced."

~ Sonya Gavankar, Broadcast Journalist, Face of the Newseum

"Underlying Michael Houlihan and Bonnie Harvey's personable writing style are the distilled experiences of two savvy entrepreneurs—lessons learned the hard way, and graciously shared by Bonnie and Michael in their valuable, and refreshingly honest, *The Barefoot Spirit*."

~ Gil Mansergh, Syndicated Film Columnist; Host & Producer,
KRCB-FM's *Word by Word: Conversations with Writers*

"Michael and Bonnie's book is a must read for anyone who is looking to start a business that will make it in today's economy. Whether you are starting a company from scratch or investing your money or someone else's, *The Barefoot Spirit* illustrates the hands on and no cost best practices that will make your company a success."

~ Andrea Keating, Founder & CEO, Crews Control

"As an entrepreneur, publicist, and publisher, I found great insight in *The Barefoot Spirit*. Michael Houlihan and Bonnie Harvey's tips on how to survive on less than a shoestring are clever, practical, and best of all, provide a good giggle to any entrepreneur in panic mode. This book is one that I'm already recommending to my readers, colleagues, and clients in start-up mode—as well as those who are ready to take their business to the next level. Here's to going Barefoot!"

~ Hope Katz Gibbs, Publisher, *Be Inkandescent* Magazine

"...a *New York Times* Bestseller and a must for any small business owner."

~ Carmen Carrozza, Business and Life Coach;
Radio Host, *Forward Motion*

"It was absolutely fantastic meeting you and Bonnie here in Kansas City! The book was amazing (a word I very sparingly use) and it was very informative while keeping a light-hearted easy to read tone."

~ Eze Redwood, Partner, Wings Cafe;
Director of Strategic Development, U-Hoops LLC

About the Authors

Michael Houlihan and Bonnie Harvey co-authored the *New York Times* bestselling business book *The Barefoot Spirit: How Hardship, Hustle, and Heart Built America's #1 Wine Brand*. The book, selected as recommended reading in the CEO Library for *CEO Forum*, chronicles Barefoot's journey from its start in the laundry room of a rented Sonoma County farmhouse in 1986 to the board room of E&J Gallo, where the brand was successfully sold in 2005. Barefoot is now the largest bottled wine brand in the world.

From the start, with virtually no money and no wine industry experience, they employed innovative ideas to overcome obstacles and create new markets and strategic alliances, while also pioneering Worthy Cause Marketing and performance-based compensation.

Since selling the brand to E&J Gallo, they consult with Fortune 500s and other companies, helping them establish and strengthen entrepreneurial company cultures through seminars, webinars, and onsite training, and travel the world speaking to corporations, conferences, symposiums, and universities. They are regular media guests and contributors to international publications and professional journals, along with being FOX News Radio Network's Workplace Culture Experts.

Houlihan and Harvey's story is widely used as a case study in schools of entrepreneurship. They were the keynote speakers at the 2014 World Conference on Entrepreneurship in Dublin, Ireland and recipients of the 2014 Distinguished Entrepreneurship Speaker Award from The Turner School of Entrepreneurship and Innovation at Bradley University. This book, *The Entrepreneurial Culture: 23 Ways to Engage and Empower Your People,* is a companion to *The Barefoot Spirit* written specifically for the C-Suite. Both books will be featured in the premiere episode and network launch of Jeff Hayzlett's C-Suite TV and C-Suite Book Club in September 2014.

Michael and Bonnie coauthor weekly no-nonsense business blogs at TheBarefootSpirit.com and TheBrandAuthority.net. For more information, contact Info@TheBarefootSpirit.com.

The Barefoot Spirit

TheBarefootSpirit.com
Info@TheBarefootSpirit.com
Twitter: @barefoot_spirit
Facebook: Facebook.com/BarefootWineFounders

Obtain your copy of the companion book, the *New York Times* business bestseller *The Barefoot Spirit: How Hardship, Hustle, and Heart Built America's #1 Wine Brand*, at TheBarefootSpirit.com.

Notes